Introduction to Folklore
Traditional Studies in Europe and Elsewhere

Ronald M. James

with illustrations by the author

Figure 1 (title page) Bas Relief from Aquae Sulis. Cover image: Often described as a Medusa, this stone bas relief is from Aquae Sulis, Bath, England. A full discussion is offered in Chapter 9.

Copyright © 2014 Ronald M. James
Reissued with revisions, 2017
All rights reserved.

ISBN: 9781521423264

In memory of my mentor,
Sven Samuel Liljeblad (1899-2000)

Contents

	Preface and Acknowledgments	vii
Chapter 1	Definitions	1
Chapter 2	How to Study Folklore	10
Chapter 3	Belief	17
Chapter 4	Calendar and Time-Related Customs	26
Chapter 5	Special Places and Times of Life	41
Chapter 6	Divination and Witchcraft	47
Chapter 7	Stories from Ancient Times	52
Chapter 8	Stories from Pre-Industrial Europe	60
Chapter 9	Supernatural Beings	72
Chapter 10	Christianization, Industrialization, and Immigration	92
Chapter 11	Urban Folklore and the Most Recent Chapter	105
Appendix 1	Folklore and Nationalism	113
Appendix 2	Folklore, Myth, and Literature	120
Appendix 3	The "Real" Events Inspiring Legends	122
Bibliography		125
Index		134

Preface and Acknowledgements

The following is adapted from Sven S. Liljeblad's *Introduction to Folklore*, which he self-published with a photocopier in 1966. Sven understood that he needed a concise overview of traditional European folklore studies for his students and that he was not likely to find a publisher for his notes, assembled from his lectures without citation. In 1978, he taught folklore for the last time, and he used his *Introduction*. Because Sven was not a native speaker of English, his *Introduction* – like his lectures – required some translation into the sort of English that late-twentieth-century American students could understand. I was his teaching assistant for that class, so I provided students with additional information and "translations" when needed.

As Sven's last student – I studied directly under his supervision from 1976 to 1981 and continued to consult with him into the late 1990s – I am able to understand sometimes ill-defined references made in his original *Introduction*. As was natural for someone who had studied folklore for over half a century, Sven sometimes made shorthand allusions to information he assumed was understood by his readers. But this was not always the case, particularly as new generations of students appeared who were further removed from the traditional roots of pre-industrial Europe and who lacked a shared vocabulary and a 1920s-definition of cultural literacy.

When I began teaching folklore classes, beginning in 1980, I drew heavily from Sven's *Introduction*, finally providing my own, amended photocopied version of the manual. But it eventually became clear that the text needed many more additions and changes if it were to be useful to modern students. The result was a handout that was a hybrid between Sven's and my own work. After Sven died in 2000 just short of his 101st birthday, I corresponded with his widow, Astrid Liljeblad (1909-2010), telling her that I was reworking Sven's *Introduction*. Astrid was enthusiastic about my efforts, wanting to see Sven's legacy survive into the new century. She hoped that I would publish my new *Introduction to Folklore* in his honor, but as the years passed, it seemed that a conventional publisher might not be the answer. I resolved, consequently, to use e-publishing for this book, to make it available to the largest possible audience at the lowest cost.

It is with all of this in mind that I dedicate this work to my mentor, Sven Samuel Liljeblad. He was both brilliant and kind. Sven emerged in the late 1920s as a prominent folklorist, linguist, and anthropologist. Eventually, he participated in an important chapter of Great Basin Native American studies beginning in the 1940s.

Born in Jönköping in southern Sweden in 1899, Liljeblad earned his doctorate at Lund University in 1927 under the direction of famed folklorist, Carl Wilhelm von Sydow (1878-1952; the father of the actor, Max von Sydow). Liljeblad's dissertation dealt with a complex of folktales involving the motif of the Grateful Dead. He and von Sydow intended the publication to be a vehicle to demonstrate a new approach to folklore studies, called the Ecotype method or the "Swedish" School (Sven and his mentor spelled it "Oicotype").

The approach of Liljeblad and von Sydow diverged from the older Finnish Historic Geographic method by placing greater emphasis on the geographic character of oral tradition rather than on its historic roots. Liljeblad drew inspiration from the work of Franz Boas (1858-1942) whose meticulous collection of Native American artifacts considered geographic variations to understand the dynamics of culture. Similarly, the Ecotype method compared differences in oral tradition to material culture, including house and oven types, to define large zones of cultural patterns (distinct from linguistic or political borders).

Liljeblad's research took him to Norway, Germany, Czechoslovakia, Finland, and Ireland, and he published in six languages before he was thirty. During the late 1920s, he organized the Swedish folklore archive at Uppsala. He then used his experience to help establish the archive of the Department of Irish Folklore in Dublin in 1929. Liljeblad wrote extensively in the 1920s and 1930s, teaching at Lund until 1936.

In the early 1930s, Liljeblad mentored German folklorist, Elisabeth Hartmann (later Hofelich-Hartmann), as she wrote what became the definitive study of Scandinavian troll beliefs, published in 1936. With the rise of Fascism in Germany during the 1930s, he participated in an underground organization operating from Copenhagen, which rescued political dissidents and Jewish refugees from Nazi oppression. After a series of events that anticipated the outbreak of war, Hartmann was summoned home, and Liljeblad's position became precarious. Initially, he planned to relocate to Afghanistan and taught himself Pashtun. Upon winning an Anders Zorn fellowship from the Swedish-American Foundation, however, Liljeblad came to the United States in 1939.

Initially, Liljeblad went to the University of California at Berkeley to work with Robert Lowie (1883-1957) and A. L. Kroeber (1876-1960). They suggested that the Swedish scholar's abilities might be best applied to the recordation of Northern Paiute, Bannock, and Shoshone oral traditions and language. After an initial foray into the Great Basin, Liljeblad participated in the war effort by teaching European culture and languages, including Finnish and Russian, to United States military personnel. In 1945, he accepted a two-year appointment at Harvard, where he met Astrid von

Heijne (1909-2010), who became his wife in 1949. Other academic affiliations included appointments at Indiana University and the University of Chicago.

Liljeblad returned to the Great Basin in the late 1940s, initially taking a professorship at Idaho State University, Pocatello and then conducting work at the University of Nevada, Reno. At the latter, Liljeblad accepted a position as the Hilliard Distinguished Professorship from 1976 until 1983. His extensive work in Great Basin linguistics and traditions became a cornerstone of articles that appear in the Smithsonian, *Handbook of North American Indians, Volume 11: Great Basin* (1986), and his work also survives in a dictionary, *The Northern Paiute-Bannock Dictionary* (2011) , compiled by Catherine Fowler and Glenda Powell, who granted Liljeblad posthumous co-authorship.

Liljeblad's work in the Great Basin spanned five decades. His legacy includes one of the largest collections of Northern Paiute, Bannock, and Shoshone language and oral tradition. Liljeblad worked at a pivotal time when much would have been lost had he not recorded the words of people throughout the region.

Before returning to Sweden in 1991, Liljeblad donated his extensive research material to the Special Collections Library at the University of Nevada, Reno. He and Astrid also established the Liljeblad Endowment at the University of Nevada, Reno, to help fund research into linguistics and folklore. In 1991, Liljeblad became the second winner of the Michael Prize at the Ljungby Oral Story Festival in Sweden, an award given to promoters of the study of oral traditions. In 1992, he was recognized as an Honorary Member of the Shoshone Paiute Tribes at the Duck Valley Reservation in Owyhee, Nevada. Earlier, in 1979, the Nevada Humanities Committee commissioned the renowned anthropologist Clifford Geertz to give a lecture in recognition of Liljeblad's career and achievements. These are only three of the many honors bestowed on the Swedish scholar. In response to his award in 1979, Sven commented to this author that "when they start giving you awards, it is time to leave." Sven Liljeblad was unpretentious.

By way of acknowledgements and besides recognizing Sven's importance to the development of this book, I thank my numerous students over the years who asked insightful questions and helped me develop this *Introduction* in response to our discussions. Similarly, discussions on the Internet, under the umbrella of "Reddit" and particularly under the "subreddits" known as "AskHistorians," "AskAnthropology," and "Mythology" provided extensive comments as I floated sections of the text to an international audience. My son, Reed, always plays an important role since he allows no assumption to be untested without numerous questions. And of course, my beloved wife, Susan, who is a brilliant historian and editor, helped immensely in developing this text.

Chapter 1 Definitions

It's the same with our modern folklorists: only buildings, tools, and customs seem to be interesting. – Elisabeth Hofelich-Hartmann (1912-2004), writing from Stuttgart, Germany, 2002.

The first place to start a discussion about folklore is with definitions. This is necessary, ironically, because folklorists and the people they study sometimes use various terms in dramatically different ways. The need for a workable definition is, at the outset, especially pivotal for the word "folklore." Although people may intuitively know what this means, professional folklorists have been unable to agree on precise language to explain what the term describes. Definitions are different from individual to individual and from place to place, and the meaning of words can change over time. The controversy over definitions reveals a great deal about the history of the field and some of the difficulties it faces as a discipline.

Part of the problem with defining "folklore" comes down to whether the word refers to a subject matter or a method of study. The term was invented by William Thoms (1803-1885) in 1846 who proposed, as he put it, that "Popular Antiquities, or Popular Literature … would be most aptly described by a good Saxon compound, Folklore, – the Lore of the People…." (Dundes, 1965) Thoms was proposing that his peers recognize the collective traditions of the common folk of the United Kingdom, but by "common," he did not mean the average person on the street. The concern of the day was that industrialization, or modernization as it is sometimes called, was transforming society, permanently changing rural, agricultural life. Traditions that had the appearance of being centuries if not millennia old were disappearing. This disturbed Thoms and many others, who hoped the term "folklore" would bring focus to a subject matter that warranted attention.

Even before Thoms made his proposal to an English audience, two German scholars had virtually invented the academic approach to the study of popular oral traditions. Jacob and Wilhelm Grimm (1785-1863 and 1786-1859, respectively) had published their first volume of *Kinder und Hausmärchen (Children's and House Folktales)* in 1812 and their *Deutsche Sagen (Teutonic Legend)* from 1816 to 1818. A series of books written independently by Jacob Grimm earned him the title of the father of folklore science. He published *Deutsche Grammatik (Teutonic Grammar)* between 1819 and 1837, and his *Deutsche Mythologie (Teutonic Mythology)* appeared in 1835. All of this happened before Thoms wrote his essay, and so clearly his invention of the term "folklore" did not occur without a context. Indeed, German and Scandinavian scientists, many the direct intellectual heirs of Jacob Grimm, would continue to shape the field of folklore studies, internationally, throughout the nineteenth century

Part of what inspired the Grimm Brothers was the need to identify a common Germanic folk culture. At the beginning of nineteenth century, Germany consisted of dozens of small, weak, independent states, and Napoleonic France seemed poised to obliterate Germany, militarily, culturally, and linguistically. Like Thoms, the Grimm brothers recognized that a changing world was devouring timeless traditions, but these young scholars also felt that the preservation of traditions could help their beloved German culture to survive the challenges it faced. Other countries would adopt their methods, but the inspiration varied. Nonetheless, many of the best folklore archives in Europe exist today where people sought to link folk ethnicity with a nationalist movement.

The term folklore originally referred to the traditions of the European peasant, but not necessarily to the study of that material. During the nineteenth century, much of Europe's peasantry were still confined by a nearly medieval illiteracy, and yet antiquarians felt they preserved the crown jewels of a nation's heritage. For enthusiasts such as Thoms, folklore meant simply the collective traditions of the people. As academic attention increasingly focused on this material, the term folklore came to mean the field of study for this subject.

Parallel to the emergence of folklore as an academic discipline was the development of ethnography. The simultaneous birth of the two academic fields caused many of the difficulties in defining folklore. Webster's dictionary describes folklore as "the traditional beliefs, legends, customs, etc., of a people" and as "the study of such lore." It defines ethnography as "a branch of anthropology dealing with the scientific description of individual cultures." A problem occurs because there is little to distinguish "culture" from "traditional beliefs, legends, customs, etc." In short, folklore and ethnography examine virtually the same thing, at least in the simplest terms. Folklorists are left to give their field distinction by insisting that either their methodology or subject matter is unique. There has been little agreement in the discipline regarding the best approach to define the exclusive turf of folklore. When Funk and Wagnalls published its *Standard Dictionary of Folklore, Mythology and Legend* in 1949, it could not find consensus on the meaning of the term folklore. It consequently offered twenty-one individually-authored definitions and left the reader to sort out the differences.

Initially, folklorists found distinction in the fact that they studied their own European traditions, while ethnographers examined other cultures, namely those that Europeans were encountering in the rest of the world. This is an awkward place to draw the line separating the two because it implies that the oral traditions of other people are somehow different from those of Europeans, and no credible scholar could promote such a concept.

Regardless of how unclear the distinction may be, the historical reality is that the two academic disciplines developed in a manner that was both parallel and independent. The result is that today folklorists examine much of the same subject that concerns ethnographers, but they use subtly different techniques. Differences include the fact that ethnographers tend to shun the study of one's own people, while folklorists encourage it. In addition, folklorists tend to place emphasis on oral traditions in a way that exceeds the approach of ethnography. Still, folklorists have recently placed greater emphasis on other aspects of culture, and as ethnographers apply themselves comprehensively to a wide variety of human behavior including oral traditions, the distinction between the disciplines is less clear. Folklorists rigorously organize and compare many aspects of oral traditions with a well-developed bibliography to assist in the task. Unfortunately, some academic folklore programs turn away from this aspect of the discipline's heritage, further blurring the distinction between folklore and ethnography.

All of this makes it extremely difficult to arrive at a definition of folklore that sets it apart from ethnography. If we fall back on Webster, we find it most simply stated. Folklore is "the traditional beliefs, legends, customs, etc., of the people," and it is "the study of such lore." It is, after all, what the folk knew to be true all along, and perhaps it is best left at that.

European folklorists, following the lead of the folk themselves, have long recognized two forms of oral tradition, *Sagen* and *Märchen*, legends and folktales. While there are many other forms of oral tradition, legends and folktales stand in opposition to one another, yet share a great deal. In reality, lines can blur.

Legends – or *Sagen* as the profession often prefers – are generally short, single-episodic stories told chiefly in the daytime. More importantly, the teller intended the listener to believe the story. Legends often have horrible ending to underscore the story's important message. Many them are, after all, meant to be instructive, to serve as warnings in some way. These types of stories are not necessarily long-lived. Their point is to reinforce and prove the legitimacy of a belief. Nonetheless, some legends take on a traditional character, can become multi-episodic, and migrate over considerable spans of time and space.

Folktales – or *Märchen*, again using the German, technical term – are longer stories with more than one episode. They are restricted, in theory at least, to evening presentation. A folktale is not to be believed, taking place in a fantastic setting. The European folktale also requires a happy ending, the cliché of "happily ever after." Any given folktale can be told with considerable variation, but they are traditional in basic form, and folklorists have spent decades tracing the history and distribution of these stories.

A word here about the term "fairytale" is appropriate. At the end of the eighteenth century, various writers, most prominently the Grimm brothers, began publishing children's stories based on folktales. These collections became extremely popular, particularly among the urban and increasingly literate emerging middle class as it found itself removed from the peasant soil that served as home to the stories. Fairytales often cause misunderstandings. In a culture that knows more about fairytales than *Märchen*, people assume that the folktale was intended for children. This is certainly not the case since the stories were often violent or sexual in ways thought inappropriate for children. Indeed, the telling of a folktale was usually delayed until the children had gone to bed. While fairytales provide the modern reader with the easiest access to the many stories that were once told internationally, one should always realize that they are removed from the primary inspiration. The original stories and their content provided serious entertainment for adults and they were part of an oral tradition, not something that was fossilized in writing.

The evolution of published fairytales had a profound effect on the popular idea of fairies, elves, trolls, and similar entities. Because fairytales became the literary domain of children, many people – including later writers – assumed the same was true of the supernatural beings. In their original context, nothing could be further from the truth. These were not cute, diminutive creatures whose sole purpose was to delight children. They were powerful, dangerous, and capable of great harm. The European peasantry feared and respected them, and their stories underscore this, conveying in uncompromising terms the code of ethics and behavior that one must employ to survive an encounter with the dangerous world of magic and power.

The definition proposed here for "fairytale" does not necessarily coincide with how people – and even some folklorists – use the term. Some scholars regard "fairytale" as appropriate for the more fantastic expressions of folktales as they were told by the folk. The reason why the term is not used in that capacity here is because the folk did not refer to these stories as fairytales and because the term implies a degree of innocence that is inappropriate; again, "fairytale" is most suitably reserved for the published children stories that gave literary expression to the adult oral fictions of the folk.

Besides the legend and the folktale, there is also the folk ballad, a specialized form of oral tradition that, like the others, incorporated a wide range of beliefs. The ballad had roots in medieval Europe, combining narrative and song. The ballad usually focused on a single incident, and it almost always emphasizes action.

Something also needs to be said here about myth. People use this term awkwardly. In a European context, myths tend to be the artificial constructs of ancient and Classical-era priests or literate people who sought to weave folk traditions into a comprehensive whole. The exercise often had political purposes, designed to provide diverse people with a single set of beliefs and stories. By reconciling similar traditions, the shared culture of these groups could be seen as more important than the differences, justifying the central rule of the king and his priests. Myth is also a way of organizing and reconciling folk traditions, which by their nature can be contradictory and highly localized. Myth tends, however, to make gods of supernatural beings, giving those powerful entities a status – for modern readers – similar to the Judeo-Christian-Islamic God, even when this comparison is not justified. Of course, it is also important to point out that myths were stories that were told – and then written down – and they were different from religion itself. Many myths were simply the shared cultural inheritance of a group of people.

In general, the word myth is best set aside when discussing more recent folk traditions, recognizing its proper status as a literary genre. Nonetheless, ancient documents recording myths can assist in understanding the history of various stories and beliefs. The authors of these texts were, after all, the first folklorists, and they were the only ones coming close to practicing the craft at the time.

Some folklorists carelessly use the term myth to denote those legends that deal with a fantastic, remote time. This primal era saw the creation of many familiar things such as day and night, fire, animals, people, mountains, and all other aspects of the present world. Folklorists properly refer to these stories as etiological legends explaining the origin of things. Sometimes, however, people interchange etiological legends with the word myth. The problem with this is that "myth" can imply something that is inherently wrong, linked to "primitive" superstitious beliefs. When the term "myth" is used for the folklore of existing cultures or for the traditions that were viable only a generation or more ago, it can take on an insulting, derogatory tone. It is best to reserve the word "myth" for ancient and Classical-era texts.

Several other terms in folklore require definition. Carl Wilhem von Sydow devised the term "fict" for a type of narrative that adults do not believe but which they tell children for various reasons, with the intent to be believed. Adults consider the boogey man to be fictitious, for example, but they used it to scare children into good behavior. The term "boogey" is apparently a nineteenth-century term related to a Celtic word, which manifests in several forms including *bucca*, a supernatural being that was taken seriously by adults and children alike. But when removed from its rural, pre-modern context, the *bucca* became the boogey man, a device used by adults to conjure up the image of a creature that presumably would punish bad children. This source of terror frequently took on various forms over time, becoming Cromwell in Ireland (a reference to Oliver Cromwell, scourge of Catholic Ireland in the seventeenth century) and Napoleon in England (after the beginning of the nineteenth century). Modern American ficts include the tooth fairy and Santa Claus. The idea of the stork bringing babies is a medieval fict that remains in today's vocabulary. This tradition is directly related to medieval traditions regarding childbirth and is discussed below.

Type, in the context of oral narrative, refers to a distinct story whether in folktale, legend, or ballad. Thus, the stories of Cinderella, Sleeping Beauty, and Snow White and the Seven Dwarfs, each represents distinct types of folktales. Folklorists have invested considerable effort identifying all the recorded versions of various types of oral narrative to arrive at their histories. There are over one thousand types of folktale identified in European tradition. Folklorists have given less attention to legends and how they appear as types, and as indicated, legends do not always fall into traditional types. Nonetheless, there are clearly hundreds if not thousands of types of this narrative form as well.

In most forms of oral narrative (folktales, legends, and ballads, for example) folklorists use the terms motif and variant. A motif is the smallest element of oral narrative. Cinderella's glass slipper, the elfin theft of a baby, or the idea that dwarfs mine underground are all motifs. There are tens of thousands of motifs, and an imaginative storyteller would creatively dip into the well to add material to the telling of a story.

A variant is a distinct version of a folktale, legend, or ballad. For example, a folktale in one area might have the hero helping a trapped animal. The creature then rewards the hero with a hair that conveys, when the hero rubs it, the power to transform into that animal's form. When the folktale type migrates to a region where people do not believe in the ability of people to turn into animals, the folktale will likely assume a new form, or variant. This new version may have the hero rubbing the hair to summon the animal for help. Perhaps the people telling the folktale will discard the motif of the animal altogether and introduce the motif of the dead helper, also known as the grateful dead, the spirit of a man whose neglected corpse is buried by the hero. Each of these choices would result in different variants, which folklorists then collect, catalogue, and analyze to understand the history of the oral narrative in question as well as the effect each culture has on a diffusing tale.

In a discussion of Classical myth and the oral traditions of Europe, it is important to understand something of the Indo-European languages. The exact nature of the Indo-European expansion is a matter of continuous debate. During the nineteenth century, linguists devoted a great deal of time exploring similarities in the group of languages known originally as Indo-Germanic. They quickly identified Latin (and its Romance-language descendants), Greek, Slavic, and the Germanic languages, including English, as part of a common linguistic family. It was easy to add to this Farsi, the language of Iran, and Sanskrit, the language of the ancient Aryan invaders of India. Indo-Germanic was, therefore, a large linguistic group that extended from India to the Germanic world. Later, it was clear that the Celtic languages of Ireland, Scotland, Wales, Cornwall, the Isle of Man, and Brittany were also part of the family, and so linguists changed the name to Indo-European to reflect the larger domain. Other languages have also been added, but this forms the basic core of what we now know as the Indo-European languages.

There is, however, controversy regarding what this linguistic distribution means. The original theory held that there was a prehistoric diaspora of the Indo-European people from central Eurasia sometime before or after the beginning of the second millennium BCE. These warrior herders presumably invaded various parts of Eurasia, conquering the local inhabitants and imposing their language and mythology wherever they went. This idea first became discredited for political reasons because Adolph Hitler exploited what many found to be a repugnant notion of racial superiority. In his mind, blond, blue-eyed Aryans demonstrated their superiority by subjugating "lesser peoples" in a distant past.

Figure 1. First-century sculpture from Homesteads on Hadrian's Wall. The Roman-era image refers to the local Celtic religion. These are three manifestations of the same god, Genii Cucullati, the hooded deities of healing, fertility, and the afterlife. Many people who spoke Indo-European were pre-occupied by the number three, and their deities frequently appear as trinities. Of all the European groups, this was most true of the Celts.

After World War II, many scholars began to question whether people were migrating or if the spread of Indo-European languages and oral traditions merely indicated the diffusion of language and folklore without the movement of people. The recent history of the English language demonstrates that language, free of people, can spread. When people from Japan and Thailand meet to discuss a business transaction, they communicate with a shared language, which is often English, and all of this occurs without anyone of English ancestry present. Similarly, Christianity conquered Europe and the New World without people from the Middle Eastern homeland migrating with it. Islam converted large parts of sub-Saharan Africa and Southeast Asia without the migration of Arabs, and Buddhism spread to China and Japan without the presence of people from India. Aspects of culture as important as language and religion can and do move independently of people. Still, sometimes people also move in large numbers, often with violent results. Europeans migrated to and conquered vast parts of the New World, Africa, and Australia, although with varying long-term effects. Arabs swept across North Africa. Germanic tribes moved into large parts of the Roman Empire, often imposing their language.

We may never know what the dispersion of Indo-European languages represented. It probably signified a combination of the spread of language and mythology and of people themselves. The number of people involved may have been limited in some areas and more plentiful in others. From a folklorist's point of view, the significance of this diffusion resides in the fact that people who spoke Indo-European languages seemed also to share – if at times unevenly – a pantheon of gods and supernatural beings, the names of which are often linguistically related. In addition, there is a common heritage of folktales from India to Ireland that seems to underscore a mutual patrimony. Since oral traditions diffuse without the movement of actual people, the resolution of the question about the spread of Indo-European languages and its relationship to the dispersal of people is of lesser importance to a discussion of folklore.

Chapter 2 How to Study Folklore

For nearly two centuries academics have debated about the best way to study oral tradition. Early folklorists could agree that documentation was critical. Modernization – the transformation of the former agrarian society into an industrial, literate, urban world – was destroying the old ways. Folklorists during the nineteenth and early twentieth centuries were involved in an increasingly urgent rescue mission, attempting to retrieve information that was quickly disappearing.

The period of emergency recordation of folklore is now all but finished for preindustrial European-based folklore. To a certain extent, however, the need may have been something of an illusion since the folk commonly praise their predecessors as better storytellers, as keepers of a richer tradition, and as more prone to believe in supernatural beings. This way of viewing previous generations may predate modernization. Regardless of the degree to which previous generation had richer, older traditions, collection today focuses on the transformation of old traditions and the birth of new ones. Folklorists who study current traditions examine how they survive and change in a modern, sophisticated world. How to analyze this material, whether old or new, is the subject of the following.

The second generation after Jacob Grimm organized what is called the Finnish Historic Geographic method for the study of the folktale. The recommended process was to collect all possible variants of a folktale type to determine the geographic distribution of variants. The folklorist then sought to determine the history of that tale type. There was an assumption that the folktale spread from a point of origin like the ripples in a pond caused by dropping a stone into the water. The circular wave farthest from the point of origin is the oldest while the waves closer to the center are younger. In the same way, folklorists looked for a point of origin somewhere near the center of the folktale's distribution. The variants farthest from the point of origin were regarded as closest to the original form, while variants at the center were presumably younger.

Folklorists began to have serious questions about this approach beginning in the 1920s. Changes in the philosophical stance of ethnography affected folklore studies. Franz Boas (1858-1942) and Bronislaw Malinowski (1884-1942) sought to develop scientific methods for the study of humanity. These involved the detailed collection of all cultural attributes followed by a rigorous analysis of the material as it exists today. Boas focused on the geographic distribution of cultural elements including aspects of material culture, and this became an inspiration for some folklorists.

During the early twentieth century, there was a shift in the way people felt humanity could be studied. In the nineteenth century, many scholars believed it was possible to understand aspects of culture and its past intuitively by studying all the available material. There was an assumption that certain basic truths would become apparent while considering history because the past merely echoes fundamental principles of humanity played out repeatedly and ingrained within the minds of all people. This approach fell into disfavor in the twentieth century as more scholars placed value on the scientific method. Intuition had no place with this new generation of positivists, academics who applied scientific method to the study of humanity.

Positivists in the early twentieth century questioned the legitimacy of attempting to understand the history of the folktale. The first critics of the Finnish method still recognized the importance of comprehensively collecting and examining the distribution of a folktale type and there was continued interest in defining the history of oral tradition. This approach emphasized geography more than history. For a positivist, it is best to study the material one can gather first hand in a scientific manner. To delve into the past is a murky process that a positivist sees as filled with subjectivity that cannot be scientifically verified.

One of the first major breaks with the Finnish method occurred in Sweden under the direction of Carl Wilhelm von Sydow. He and his students developed what came to be called the Oicotype method or Swedish School – which appears here as Ecotype, adopting an English spelling of the term. It took its name from a principle in biology, which states that as a species of plant diffuses, it can manifest differently in various environments. Applying this method to folklore called for the comparative study of variants of folktales and legends to determine if they had commonly-shared boundaries. The Ecotype method borrowed heavily from Boas who was using a similar approach for the study of American Indian culture. The goal of von Sydow was to determine geographic distributions of aspects of folklore ranging from oral tradition to house types, oven types, and other components of material culture. He and his students hoped to develop a holistic approach to folklore that could be verified scientifically. They surmised that culture boundaries occurred in response to ancient forces. Ultimately, it was not possible to determine whether these divisions were a matter of environment, some Neolithic distribution of groups, or some other factor (each of these were proposed at one time or another), but the cause was not the central focus of the approach.

The greatest attack on the Finnish method, however, came from a scholar in the Soviet Union, but the ramifications of his work would not be felt for several decades. Vladímir Propp was a folklorist in the former Soviet Union who took a radically different look at oral tradition, again influenced by the positivists. Propp's 1928 publication of the *Morfológija skázki* (*Morphology of the Folktale*) suggested that the concept of the folktale type was an illusion. For Propp and his structuralism, there were no traditional types passing through time with variants manifesting in diverse places. He suggested that a basic format, a set of rules, governed the telling of all folktales. A storyteller would simply follow the rules, picking from a vast menu of motifs. Because there were rules and a set number of motifs, the same stories would eventually reappear, but they were not necessarily linked historically. For Propp, what appeared to be a system organized as types was an illusion.

Propp's interpretation was particularly well suited to the Soviet Union. The Finnish method – and even the Ecotype method – maintained that long ago some imaginative storyteller invented a folktale that diffused over time. This perspective ennobled each folktale type, suggesting that most peasant storytellers were merely vessels who passed on an ancient story, the expression of someone else's great artistry. For Propp, every storyteller had the potential for creativity. A storyteller might repeat a tale previously told, but the narrator could just as easily invent a new story, drawing on motifs and employing the accepted structure of the folktale genre. This interpretation was appropriate for egalitarian ideals of Soviet society, but this is not to dismiss the conclusion simply because it fit in with a political doctrine.

Propp's work remained untranslated for several decades; politics did not encourage the diffusion of ideas across the Soviet border during the 1930s. At the same time, madmen used the Finnish method for their own diabolical purposes: Hitler's racism drew strength from the idea of an ancient Indo-European culture that was purely Aryan, only to be debased and polluted through contact with other people. The idea that folklorists could delve into the past and reconstruct an ancient Teutonic mythology was extremely attractive to Hitler and his followers.

The preoccupations of fascists caused some folklorists to brand attempts to reconstruct the origins of a folktale as somehow inherently racist. This unfortunate link coincided with the growing inclinations of positivists to discredit attempts at historical analysis. After World War II, many folklorists sought a new approach. The Finnish method survived, but it was wounded. Ironically, this was also the period of the most substantial international contribution to the Finnish method. Stith Thompson at the University of Indiana published his revised and enlarged edition of the *Motif-Index of Folk-Literature* in 1955, and he then released his updated version of Antti Aarne's *The Types of the Folktale* in 1961. These were not in any way linked to fascism; the thorough documents were attempts to mold the Finnish approach to positivist ideals. Still, many American folklorists, in particular, looked in other directions for inspiration.

In 1958, Svatava Pirkowa-Jakobson and Lawrence Scott edited and translated Propp's essay into English, striking a chord that fit the time. Internationally, folklore was ready for a change because of positivism, because of the fascists, and because the tired question of origins was not yielding adequate results in the eyes of many. North America was especially ripe for conversion. Lacking much by way of ancient traditions (aside from those of Native Americans), American folklorists were interested in the dynamic process of creativity. In addition, the combined effect of European fascism and liberal academics drew many American folklorists to an approach that seemed based on the egalitarianism of Karl Marx. Propp was immediately fashionable in many circles for political and philosophical reasons.

Fashionable is one thing; accurate is another. Ultimately, we must ask whether Propp's approach fits the evidence. One major criticism of Propp's concept of independent invention is that for years folklorists have asked storytellers for original folktales. When offered large amounts of money for newly-created stories, even the most gifted narrators have had to refuse the invitation, stating invariably that folktales are traditional things to be repeated, but they cannot be invented. It appears, in fact, that the invention of a folktale is extremely rare rather than an on-going process.

Some societies, however, may treat the material in a more flexible, inventive way. Alan Dundes (1934-2005) in his path-finding *Morphology of North American Indian Folktales* (1964) found that details of various stories frequently changed from one telling to the next, even when told by the same narrator. There is less evidence of this sort of flexibility with European material, but even there, the option of changing folktales cannot be dismissed as non-existent. Cornish droll tellers, the professional storytellers of Cornwall, took pride in altering stories to suit the location and audience, changing stories in a way that might have seemed inappropriate in a place like Ireland, for example. At the same time, it is important to note that Dundes acknowledged that in some cultures –

notably those of the Southwest – the faithful transmission of stories was more common than elsewhere among American Indians.

Propp's analysis of the constant invention of the folktale may not always fit the facts, but that does not negate the validity in the concept. It is reasonable to conclude that there is an underlying structure in oral narrative, and it is worthwhile to understand this structure as thoroughly as possible. Whether the structure can operate independently of a tale type, providing the outline necessary to create similar stories repeatedly over time, is the question. Even if the answer is generally no, the underlying structure may still exist and have significance. In addition, some cultures that place less value on faithfully repeating stories as they are told may be hotbeds of creativity, guided by the rules of oral tradition, continually reinventing tales without any historical connection.

The debate over the nature of the folktale is, of course, not the only discussion about how to deal with folklore, but it played an important role in defining important issues, namely whether the material is traditional or the form is paramount. Alan Dundes published two readers that provide excellent samplers of the writings of various folklorists. His insightful introductions are particularly valuable and worth consultation. See *The Study of Folklore* (1965) and *International Folkloristics: Classic Contributions by the Founders of Folklore* (1999).

The popularity of one approach among non-folklorists warrants a digression. In the last part of the twentieth century, Joseph Campbell (1904-1987) created a great deal of interest in mythology and folklore with a series of publications on the subject. This was followed by a 1980s series of television interviews, which propelled Campbell to popularity, but not necessarily with all folklorists. To a certain extent, Campbell was relying on an older approach that Carl Gustav Jung (1875-1961) developed. Jung was a Swiss psychologist who studied with Sigmund Freud (1856-1939) but later broke with his mentor's teachings to form his own approach to the study of the human mind. Jung developed the idea of the collective unconscious, maintaining in almost spiritual terms that all of humanity is linked by archetypes that existed in an unconscious common denominator. Ultimately, Jung implied that certain themes are woven into the fabric of the universe. According to Jung, all of humanity shared a symbolic vocabulary which manifests in dreams, mythology, folklore, and literature.

Jungian psychology was extremely popular during the upheavals of the 1960s when people looked for mystical explanations of life to unify all existence. Despite the faddish qualities of the late twentieth-century consumption of Jungian ideas, it is easy to regard Jung as an exceptional thinker with an extraordinary background of diverse reading. Campbell borrowed heavily from Jung, presenting many of these ideas in an easily consumable package that, in its turn, became something of a fad during the 1980s. Campbell drew not only on Jung, but also on Otto Rank's 1932 publication, *The Myth of the Birth of the Hero*.

There are clearly many good ideas in this literature, but there are problems with the approach of Campbell, Jung, and Rank from the point of view of folklore studies. The first is that they tend to present the concept of tale types in mythology and folklore as though it were a new discovery. In other words, they ignore the highly-developed bibliography that the discipline of folklore offers. The second, more serious problem is that this line scholarship makes no distinction between the core of a story and its culturally-specific or narrator-specific variants and variations. The Jungian-Campbell approach treats any variant of a story as an expression of the collective unconscious, regardless of whether its form is the product of an individual storyteller's idiosyncrasies or of the cultural predilections of a region made irrelevant by traveling to the next valley. And with this process, all the other variants are ignored, including ones that may contradict the initial observation. This does not mean that there are no valuable insights in the work of Jung and Campbell. There are, of course, but folklorists regard their approach as removed from their own discipline and flawed, to a certain extent.

Dundes presented a similar critique of Freudian-based psychoanalysis of folktales. In his *The Study of Folklore* (1965), he wrote that "the analysis is usually based upon only one version…To comparative folklorists who are accustomed to examining hundreds of versions of a folktale or folksong before arriving at even a tentative conclusion, this apparent cavalier approach to folklore goes very much against the grain. How does the analyst know, for example, whether or not the particular version he is using is typical and representative." (107) Dundes also pointed out that often the "variant" presented by the psychological analysis is from "a children's literature anthology, rather than directly from oral tradition."

There was also a wave of pop-psychological treatments of folklore, arguing, for example, that the material is sexist in a variety of ways or that it can be transformed to provide young girls with a positive self-image. It should come as no surprise that peasant folklore from the nineteenth-century was sexist since it came from a male-dominated society. On the other hand, there is a long-held practice of re-writing folktales to suit the needs of the moment. That is exactly what the Brothers Grimm did in their effort to provide speakers of German with a national, popular literature. If there is a benefit to feminizing folktales, the effort can take its place in an honorable tradition.

In 1975, Bruno Bettelheim published *The Uses of Enchantment: The Meaning and Importance of Fairy Tales*. Bettelheim proposed that children should be reintroduced to fairytales since, he argued, this traditional body of young people's literature was extremely important to their psychological growth and well-being. His work won wide acclaim, but it is based on a flawed premise. Folktales were not told to children. It was not until Western Europe adopted the practice of transforming this material into published fairytales that children even had access to these stories. That's not to say that there is no value in reading fairytales to children. It is simply a fact that children did not traditionally hear folktales.

CHAPTER 3 BELIEF

European folklorists historically focused on several aspects of oral tradition, belief, and custom. American and recent European studies have occasionally wandered further afield, but the European bedrock provides a place to begin. Folklorists study the annual seasons and holidays; the rites of passage at birth, marriage, and death; means to cure illness and injury; witches and witchcraft; belief in supernatural beings; and oral narratives. Except for the subject of oral narrative (folktales, legends, ballads, and other genres), the rest of folklore can be grouped under the heading of belief and custom (for "custom" see chapter 4).

One of the best examples of a comprehensive look at belief and custom is the *Handwörterbuch des deutschen Aberglaubens* (*Encyclopedia of the German Popular Superstitions*), which appeared in nine volumes between 1927 and 1942. This is an exceptional work because it offers published material that most folklore archives only possess in unpublished form. A similar publication includes a wide variety of material from the Finnish collection: *Suomen kansan muinaisia taikoja* (*Old Magic Practices of the Finnish People*), which appeared in eight volumes between 1891 and 1934. The final three volumes provide an example of the degree of detail possible. There are roughly 20,000 elementary ideas and their variants concerning the magical practices associated with cattle.

In short, it would be possible to become lost in the detail. Nonetheless, an overview of various forms of belief and customs can be beneficial.

For European peasants (if not for non-industrial people in general), the world was filled with the supernatural and its potential. They believed that a wide variety of supernatural beings came and went freely about the world. This could occur any time, but nighttime, special days, and specific locations could require extra precaution. People also believed that there were magical practices one could and should undertake to protect oneself and to manipulate the supernatural to prevent calamity or to eke out a better existence. Two examples demonstrate that some traditions survive both industrialization and immigration. North Americans preserve the preventative practices of knocking on wood and throwing spilled salt over one's left shoulder (although the latter is quickly dying). Both acts were to distract the supernatural from doing harm.

Traditionally, Europeans used magic in various minor ways. Expert practitioners developed the generally accepted techniques and beliefs into a refined craft, but they did not deviate from the core beliefs of their culture. Liljeblad, in his *Introduction to Folklore*, uses ten categories to group the rules of magic. They are as follows:

1. Bodily dimensions and movements: There are choices one can make involving front and back and left and right. The front is positive, and the back is negative. Movements forward and backward have positive and negative values, respectively.

Similarly, the right hand and movements to the right are positive, and those involving the left are negative. By analogy, clockwise, a movement involving left to right, is positive and counterclockwise is negative. The direction of the sun in the Northern Hemisphere reinforces the basic assumption that left to right is the natural motion of the world.

The belief in the importance of front and back and left and right inspired day-to-day practices involving the supernatural and it dominated formal magical practices. The back of the house was particularly vulnerable to the supernatural. It required special magical attention in the form of painted symbols or other magical practices to thwart possible dangers. Movements backwards were considered malevolent. Parents told children not to walk backwards because they would "drag father and mother to hell." A person taking a few steps backward would be told "you go wrong."

Along these lines, cooks stirred food clockwise, and they cut and served from left to right. If someone turned his hand counterclockwise, he needed to turn his hand an equal number of times clockwise to undo the harm. In the same way, popular warning discouraged twisting one's thumbs around – what is called "twiddling one's thumbs" – toward oneself. They should rotate in the opposite direction. Custom forbid dancing counterclockwise, an act that would inspire the warning, "You dance against the sun. Turn around."

The right hand has traditional preference over the left, a fact reflected in language and practice. The idea that one should begin the day with the right foot out of the bed is echoed in the phrase, "he got out of bed on the wrong side today."

All this resulted in day-to-day activities that respected the perceived natural order of the world and its preference for front over back, right over left, and clockwise over counterclockwise. When wishing to manipulate the supernatural, however, the patterns were typically reversed. The left hand as well as backwards and counterclockwise motions gained importance. Walking backwards and counterclockwise around a church three times could give the power to see the future. The same act around a well, combined with throwing an object representing an illness, backward over one's left shoulder into the well, could restore health. A silver coin in the left shoe protected against evil.

These practices could quickly step into the sinister realm. Magical potions were stirred counterclockwise, particularly if something hurtful was sought. The Stations of the Cross are arranged clockwise within a Catholic church. Walking counterclockwise inside a church, backwards, then reciting the Lord's Prayer backwards at the rear of the church with one's back to the altar was sufficient to call up the devil.

By analogy with the idea of front and back, one avoided turning things upside down or inside out unless there was a specific need or desired result. When walking home in the dark, it might be wise to pull one's pockets out as a barrier against elfin attack. An intrepid soul might wear a coat inside out, thus acquiring supernatural sight to see the elves. This was not recommended since the supernatural beings frequently punished such audacity. The same act could produce different results, as described in legends, depending on the motive of the protagonist.

2. The Cardinal Points: The origins for the terms east, west, south, and north hint at an ancient posture facing east with the left side of the body to the north, the right to the south, and the back to the west. Even the word "orientation" descends from a Latin word for sunrise, and hence the east. It appears that facing east has had premier importance for centuries if not millennia, particularly when dealing with the supernatural. Most cultures share this point of view. Traditionally churches situated the altar at the east side of the long axis so that the congregation faced in that direction to view the priest and the Elevation of the Host.

The idea of facing east gave each direction a specific meaning. East (front) and south (right) had positive value, while the contrasting west and north were negative. North was a direction of disaster and unhappiness. Diseases, for example, could be magically discarded in rivers that flowed north. In medieval Scandinavia, the land of death was to the north. For the Irish, *Tir na nOg*, the land of everlasting youth (and death), was to the west. In Arthurian literature, King Arthur goes west to Avalon after receiving his mortal wound. The power of this direction gave meaning to the western islands that eighth-century Celtic monks inhabited as they awaited their final meeting with God.

3. The Phases of the Moon: According to traditional belief, the new, waxing, and full moons had the positive power of growth and energy. The waning moon was negative. Tradition held that farmers sowed fields at a new moon to insure growth similar to the extraordinary increase of the celestial object. Animals were slaughtered during the waning moon so maggots would not grow. The folk held weddings during a waxing moon, and any large undertaking was initiated during that time.

4. The Four Elements: The peasantry of medieval Europe believed the material universe consisted of four elements – earth, air, fire, and water. All things, including the living, represented a combination of these elements. In their pure form, the elements contained contrasting magical potential, both to manipulate the world and to predict the future. This idea was deeply grounded in the culture of the Middle Ages.

When someone fell ill, people often believed it was because one of the four elements within the body was out of balance. The person was ill-humored: that is, the patient's humors or bodily substances were not in the proper portions. The cure must correct the issue of balance or the illness would persist. The practice of applying leaches and of bleeding – intentionally opening veins to drain off "bad" blood – was an attempt to restore a healthy order to the four elements. Diagnostics could be difficult, however, in determining which element was actually the source of the problem. One technique employed the retrieval of stones from the earth, from a streambed, and from the roots of a tree that had emerged from the ground. The healer would heat them in a fire, then throw them into water and listen for the sounds each made for a sign as to which element was imbalanced.

5. Colors: Different cultures defined colors in various ways. Some, for example, make no distinction between blue and green. The relative meanings of colors are also different from culture to culture. For medieval European society, these meanings affected divination, dress patterns, heraldic symbolism, and the colors associated with the Church liturgy and calendar. White was believed to be the holiest. The Church used it during Christmas, Easter, and festivals associated with the Virgin Mary. Red symbolized fire, love, and blood, and the Church consequently used it during feasts of martyrs. Violet was the color of penance and was associated with Advent and Lent.

For the secular world, white symbolized hope in love, while red referred to love itself. Blue was associated with fidelity, green with immunity from love, yellow with envy, and brown with obligation in love. Black was the color of sorrow. In addition, green could signify hope or faithful love. People used these colors in dress, and it was understood as a language in itself.

The folk also used colors in magical practices. A young woman seeking information about a future spouse could find four straws growing at the same place on midsummer night. By tying pieces of yarn of different, meaningful colors to each of the straws and waiting to see how they grew, it would be possible to gain insight about the future.

In folktales, symbolic color reference could be made to the time of day. White represented morning, red stood for noon, and black signified night. A story might include, for example, incantations involving the colors that affected the hero during the corresponding times of the day.

6. Numbers and Letters. Pre-industrial cultures regarded numbers as having symbolic if not magical meaning beyond their actual numerical value. This is particularly true of numbers one through four, although some cultures ascribe meaning to numbers greater than this. The first four numbers are potent because they are often regarded as corresponding to the directions of the world, the four cardinal points. In cultures such as the Native American Navaho who recognize the zenith and nadir as being part of the cardinal directions, the first six numbers have corresponding significance.

Many cultures also regard one as the number associated with heaven and the male domain, while the number two refers to earth and the female half of the universe. For magical purposes, one is positive while two has negative meaning. One stands for life, and two for death.

In Europe, the basic use of the first numbers was expanded during the medieval period, drawing on perceived or real traditions of the ancient Babylonians and Egyptians. The Greek Pythagoreans of the sixth century, BCE also developed some of this symbolism. These philosophers were interested in the correlation of numbers, symbolism, magical powers, and the order of the universe. This idea was extremely influential for the magical practices of medieval Europe.

Various cultures throughout history have invented means of writing. Whenever this occurs, the system of writing invariably acquires magical powers beyond the literal meaning of the various symbols. The alphabet was particularly useful for magic because there were fewer symbols, and they had an agreed-upon order, whose corresponding numerical value reinforced magical meaning. Whenever most of the folk could not read, they tended to perceive literacy as having even greater power.

Using the Greek alphabet, which many Europeans saw as having magical significance, *Alpha* referred to heaven, while *Beta* signified earth or evil. It is not mere coincidence that the Semitic alphabet began with the word for "bull," that is, the very male "bull of heaven" and the second letter was "Beth," the letter "B", meaning a house or something linked with women and the earth. Furthermore, the letter "A," when placed upside down, portrays a bull's head with horns, much as it can be seen in the constellation Taurus. The letter "B," when turned to the left so its flat side rests on the bottom, depicts the two domes of a house.

Indo-Europeans were preoccupied with the number three and the belief that things naturally fell into groups of three. Because of this, *Gamma*, the third letter of the Greek alphabet, symbolized perfection and a mystical perception of heaven. *Delta*, the fourth letter, referred to the four elements.

The Germanic world of northern Europe imported the idea of an alphabet before conversion to Christianity. Germanic cultures were free to develop a system of writing independent of the Roman Empire. The Germanic letters are called runes, the order of which is known as the "futhark" (fuþark) after the first six letters. Runes were particularly well adapted for engraving. Indeed, the English word "written" derives from the Old English word *writan* meaning etched or engraved. The runic letters of the futhark had magical significance related to words associated with each letter and their numerical order. Thus, the third letter, called "thorn" (a voiceless "th" written "þ") was important in the practice of magic, particularly with negative intention. In a Christian context, the thorn represented the Devil. The "n" rune symbolized necessity and magical compulsion. The "I" rune signified coldness and death. The "e" rune represented Odin, the god of wisdom. Letters could be linked in sequence to procure a desired effect.

When Christian missionaries spread north from the Roman Empire beginning in the fourth and fifth centuries, they brought the Roman alphabet. Although the Roman alphabet replaced runes for most writing after Christianization, people performing magic retained runes as the best tools to draw on the power of the supernatural.

7. Emblems: Many other signs had special magical properties. People used various types of crosses, many of them serving as protective magic. The swastika gained ill fame because Adolph Hitler adopted it in twentieth-century Nazi Germany. Before the 1930s, however, the *swastika* was positive, drawing on the power of the four directions and the clockwise motion of the sun. Its opposite, with the arms pointing counterclockwise, was a symbol for antagonistic, hurtful magic.

The pentagram, the five-pointed star, was also once a potent symbol, and it has become one of the favorites of those seeking to revive traditional magic practices. The delta, a perfect, equilateral triangle, has always had potency because it draws on the number three and its sides are perfectly uniform.

Humanity consistently employs these emblems. Indeed, there is evidence of their use in prehistoric times.

8. Accidental contrast: Practitioners of magic looked for contrasts. Nature and circumstance provided ample opportunities that could be exploited. A female shaman would be the best choice to treat an ill man. The opposite was true for a sick woman. When practicing magic, the first and last of a series of things had potency. Thus, the first and last harvested sheaves of wheat from a field possessed special magical properties.

In addition, practitioners of magic always selected the least common means to act. When choosing between using one of two objects or when deciding whether to approach a task one way or the other, a shaman selected the least traveled course because it had the most magical potential.

9. Culturally determined contrast: People place extensive cultural prohibitions on themselves regarding what can be said and done. In postmodern America, the shock value of violating traditional prohibitions has desensitized society and broken down many time-honored barriers. Pre-industrial societies strictly defined which things were allowed and which ones were forbidden. Anthropologists often use the Polynesian terms of *noa* (allowed) and *tabu* (forbidden) because the island people of the Pacific provide excellent examples of how the widest possible array of actions could come under complicated rules of prohibition. Indeed, the Polynesian example is so well-known that the word "taboo" has found its way into common English usage.

Taboos can apply to the entire community, to a group within the community, or they can be imposed (by oneself or by others) on individuals. Irish early-medieval epics, grounded firmly in folklore, contain the concept of the *geasa*, which was a taboo that someone magically placed on another. The degree of the magic was often unspecified, extremely weak, or even non-existent, but a person under a *geasa* was obligated to follow its restrictions.

Hawaiian society developed an extensive complex of taboos. Certain foods were restricted to the royal family or to other groups. Specific words and actions were prohibited for some and required of others. Taboos could even restrict who was allowed to look at a member of the royal family. Violations could be punished in the harshest ways since the well-being of the community at large was at stake.

Shared cultural taboos might include the idea that it is improper to point at stars. Specifically naming certain mountains, animals, supernatural beings, and other things could be prohibited, particularly in their presence. Various cultures have consequently provided a range of *noa* names for various things. Anthropologists also refer to these alternative means of address as circumlocutions. A *noa* name is used under circumstances when the actual name would be taboo. Northern European bakers avoided naming the fire, but instead spoke of the heat. Butchers would not refer to blood. They replaced that word with "sweat."

The English word "bear" descends from the Proto-Germanic root *beron* meaning "brown one." This was apparently a way of avoiding the original word *rkto*, from which was related to the Latin *ursus*. In this case, prehistoric speakers of ancestral English presumably avoided the actual name until it ceased to be remembered. Ethnographic evidence from the northern latitudes indicate that one should not name the bear in its presence (that is, in the forest) or when planning to hunt for a bear. Compare, for example, Russian *medved*, which means honey eater, and Swedish *sotfot*, meaning "sweet foot." Both refer to the bear's interest in honey. Native American Shoshoni politely discuss the bear as "our father's sister."

Words applied to the supernatural beings of nature provide what appear to be additional examples of circumlocution, which are particularly pertinent for a discussion of folklore. The English word "elf" descends from a root word that apparently described a shimmering, shiny appearance. It is related to the name Alps, the Swiss mountains, and the River Elbe in Germany. Because the term "elf" originally referred to a characteristic of the supernatural beings as opposed to what had been an actual, presumably-taboo name, it would be easy to assume that this term is a circumlocution. It is possible, however, that there never was a proper name for these supernatural beings, who were simply discussed in polite, descriptive ways. Eventually, however, people forgot the original meaning of the term "elf," and as it became regarded as a proper name, various other circumlocutions including the "good neighbors" or the "fair folk" became alternatives safer than saying "elf."

Similar circumlocutions are found elsewhere, Scandinavian elves are often called *hulderfolk* or simply *huldre*, meaning the "hidden folk" or the "hidden ones." The Irish word for fairies, *sidhe* (hence, for example, banshee – woman fairy), was once a *noa* name that made reference to living in a mound. But again, there may have no taboo, proper name that was being avoided. Centuries of use have made the term *sidhe* sacred, and it is now avoided. Instead the Irish may speak of the "wee folk" or the "beautiful ones." Each culture can have a range of contrasting *noa* and taboo words, even if there are only linguistic remnants of this practice.

Besides language taboos, most cultures have a range of social, food, marriage, and kinship-related restrictions. In the context of magic, it is sufficient to say that a shaman must observe a series of taboos, both those commonly accepted in society as well as those restrictions specifically adopted by the practitioner of magic. These may include a taboo, for example, against speaking or eating before delving into one's craft of divination and magic.

10. "Choice of Two": Depending on the aim of his or her action, the practitioner of magic had a choice between two contrasts: male and female, one time or twice, the first or last of a series of things, using the right or left hand, facing east or west, walking clockwise or counterclockwise, and so forth. Someone seeking to effect magic would make choices depending on whether the magic was anti-social or regarded as helpful. Whatever was the case, the magic relied on the obvious contrasts pervasive in the world.

CHAPTER 4 CALENDAR AND TIME-RELATED CUSTOMS

Folklorists recorded a wide variety of customs when documenting the beliefs, traditions, and practices of pre-industrial European peasantry. The folk, being tied to the land and the agricultural year, spent a great deal of effort documenting the passage of time and maintaining a calendar with strictly-followed observances. The subject of time and the calendar, then, is an important place to being with a discussion of folk customs.

Ways to Address Time

1. Day and Night: The preoccupation with time, the division of the day into precisely defined hours, minutes and seconds, and the idea of changing the day at midnight are all modern practices associated with an industrial world. European peasants described time much differently. They separated the day into forenoon and afternoon. Europeans divided the night into watches, of which there were four, accounting for the time it took a night watchman in a town or a large village to make the rounds by walking around the community.

Before industrialization, most languages did not have the concept of a twenty-four-hour day, which includes both daylight and night. Words referred either to the time of daylight or night. In modern English, the word "day" is in fact used to include the time of darkness, to which it makes no literal reference. The German word *Volltag* literally means "full day," but it is a recent term that suits the need to describe the entire period of time.

For most pre-industrial people, day and night were separate, distinct terms. Time was typically counted in either "days" or "nights" or in "suns" or "sleeps." Homeric literature counts time with *eos*, the word for dawn. The English term "fortnight" refers to fourteen nights. Arabic uses a term meaning "three night," and Sanskrit has a "ten night."

Referring to a day as the time of daylight made each day longer or shorter according to the time of the year. Each successive forenoon and afternoon, consequently, were different from the previous ones. Traditionally, Europeans regarded the night before the day as being linked to it. Holidays and other days of importance consequently began the ceremony of ritual on the evening before the day. The Jewish Sabbath and holidays begin at sunset for this reason. Similarly, Halloween (the evening before All Hallows Day), Christmas Eve (the evening before Christmas), and New Year's Eve (the evening before the first day of the year) were originally tied to the day of celebration just as they are today. To the mind of the modern industrial world these evenings anticipate the day of celebration, but they were originally the beginning of the holiday.

The idea of the hour apparently first dates to ancient Sumerian and Babylonian astrologers. They divided the modern twenty-four-hour day into twelve hours. They chose the number twelve to correspond with the twelve months of the year and their corresponding signs of the zodiac. The Romans adopted this system during the first centuries of empire, but it did not take hold entirely. Egyptians contrasted with the Mesopotamian system by using twenty-four hours for the day. Medieval astrologers adopted the Egyptian approach, giving the modern world its system of time keeping. The introduction of the clock and the necessity of precise time keeping in an industrial environment made the hour a strictly-defined unit of time. None of these developments, however, occurred early enough to influence traditional European peasant culture.

2. Seasons: For many pre-industrial cultures, seasons were far more important than the concept of the 365-day year. To count the passage of years, people commonly referred to the number of a specific season that had passed. They might, for example, count years as winters. Liljeblad writes that "when asking somebody about his age, a Bannock Indian says, 'How many winters ago did you become a human being?'" In some Slavic languages, the words for "summer" and "year" are the same when considering numerous years, which were expressed by the number of summers that had passed. The Russian word *lyet*, meaning both the season and the year, is a good example of this.

The lunar cycle was also extremely important to pre-industrial people, who often paid little attention to the solar calendar. Thus, they could count the passage of time with the phases of the moon and the passages of seasons. Priests or government administrators usually led the way toward adopting a solar calendar. This was true during each of the Classical periods of civilization in Egypt, Mesopotamia, Greece, and Rome. The Church also followed this model, exporting it with conversion. Nevertheless, changing to a solar calendar was a slow process, and peasants only reluctantly adapted to this new way of viewing the passage of time.

3. The Week: The Romans, Greeks, and Egyptians did not employ a seven-day week even when they used the solar calendar. The idea of a seven-day week came from ancient Babylon making inroads into the Roman Empire after the first century. Still, Rome did not formally adopt the week until 321 CE.

People throughout the world recognize a period of time ranging from three to ten days that plays the same role as the modern week. These are frequently divisions of the lunar cycle. In agricultural societies, the week is often four to five days and is tied to markets. Central Africa, for example, has a four-day week with the market as the focus.

For the Babylonians, seven was a particularly important number. They recognized seven heavenly bodies that moved independently of the stars: what we now call Mercury, Venus, Mars, Jupiter, Saturn, the sun, and the moon. Each of these astronomical objects corresponded to a deity. In addition, much of Babylonian astrology focused on the moon, each phase of which lasts approximately seven days. It was easy, therefore, to associate each day of the week with a deity. The Romans, adopting this practice, began the week with Saturday, naming that day for Saturn, the god identified with the most remote and slowest of the visible moving planets. Days for the sun and moon followed, and then Mars, Mercury, Jupiter, and Venus had their respective days. Romance languages preserve these pagan designations.

The Germanic world imported the Roman concept of the week before Christianization, so they substituted the names of their own gods for the Roman ones. They only had, however, a four-day week, and they consequently discarded Saturday through Monday, which returned later with the Christian faith. In addition, the Germanic world did not associate celestial objects with their gods, and as a result, the designations for the days of the week had no counterpart in astrology.

Tiw/Týr, the god of war, assumed the position of Mars. Odin, god of wisdom and magic (Woden for the Anglo-Saxons), took the place of Mercury, although in both cases the analogy was weak. Thor, the Germanic sky god of thunder, was a more obvious substitute for Jupiter. Freya, goddess of love and fertility, assumed the place of Venus.

The preoccupation of the Christian calendar with the importance of Sunday as that religion's Sabbath was influenced by the popularity of a Roman religion known as Mithraism, which held the sun as sacred. For the Germanic world, Thor was generally regarded as supreme, and so Thursday assumed premier significance. The important role of Thursday, as opposed to Sunday, created an ambiguity for Northern European folk culture until industrialization and the adoption of the idea of a weekend, consecrating

Sunday as the Sabbath. In Germanic-based European folklore, the evening before Thursday or Sunday were the best time for magic. In addition, dreams during those nights had greater potential to become reality. A person born on Thursday should not be baptized on Sunday, and the opposite was also true. If this taboo were broken, the child would grow up seeing ghosts. In addition, only those born on one of those two days had the potential to become a sorcerer.

4. The Zodiac: The ancient Mesopotamians developed the concept of twelve houses of the sun through which all seven moving celestial objects traveled. The number twelve corresponds to the lunar cycles that roughly fit into the solar cycle. Because the Mesopotamian twelve houses were based on constellations, they were a truer representation of a solar year and the passage of time. The Mesopotamians referred to those twelve constellations as "the girdle of the signs," a term still used in Arabic. When the Greeks adopted the system of the twelve constellations, they called it *zodiakós*, meaning "the circle of animals."

Although the Mesopotamian week diffused with Christianity into Europe, its zodiac was slow to follow. Late medieval scholars began working with the concept by the fifteenth century, but the folk did not adopt the zodiac for another three hundred years. Printed almanacs featuring the zodiac appeared in the eighteenth century, inspiring European peasants to incorporate the symbols into magical divination practices. They also adopted the medieval scholarly speculation that the zodiac determined a person's nature according to the timing of one's birth.

5. The Popular Calendar: Throughout Europe, summer and spring festivals usually celebrate the beginning and unfolding of the agricultural season. In contrast, those of fall and winter commemorate harvest and recall pre-Christian death festivals. Specific holidays vary from culture to culture, but the following are a few highlights to serve as a brief indication of the possibilities.

Spring:

February 2. St. Brigit's Day

In ancient Ireland, early February signaled the beginning of the agricultural year. As such, it was a time when food was at a minimum. The term "February" comes from a Latin root that refers to atonement because it was a time of fasting. The beginning of February was likely sacred to the Celts as a month dedicated to the important goddess Brighid.

Figure 2. The Roman-Celtic goddess Brigantia was related to the ancient deity Brighid, the namesake of St. Brigit of Ireland. This illustration is after a statue in northern England, ca. second century, CE.

St. Brigit was the founder of a significant convent called Cill Dara, the Church of the Oak Tree, now known as Kildare. It was probably a prehistoric religious site dedicated to the goddess Brighid, and the Christian saint apparently used her pagan namesake as a way of converting and winning the support of her Irish followers.

The Irish still regard Brigit as a protector of animals, the fields, and the weak. She is often called the Mary of the Irish. It was once customary on St. Brigit's Day Eve for groups of people, particularly young girls, to go house to house singing and dancing, collecting eggs or money. The leader typically dressed as St. Brigit and carried a homemade doll called *Brídeog* (young Brigit).

Introduction to Folklore

Figure 3. Ireland's St. Brigit's Cross has prehistoric roots. Traditionally woven from straw, the form illustrated above draws on the four directions. The Irish believed that the cross had the ability to protect households. Some variants have only three arms.

For centuries, the Irish have woven Brigit's crosses out of straw and rushes. These were regarded as having tremendous power to protect, drawing on the strength of the saint. The Irish often placed a Brigit's cross in the rafters to ensure health and good fortune for the following year.

February 14. St. Valentine's Day

Many countries including England, France, and Belgium celebrated St. Valentine's Day as the first day of spring. There is also some indication that this was the day when many medieval villages convened the first annual meeting of the Young Men's Society to determine who would be allowed to court whom.

May 1. St. Walpurgis' Day/May Day

May Day has a long-standing tradition as a time to celebrate spring. The word "May" is related to the English word "might." In a *Star Wars* vocabulary, it could be translated as "the force," and this is exactly what May Day originally celebrated – the force and life power of nature. The English Maypole was a thinly-veiled attempt to commemorate the virility of the season. For central and western Europe, May Day was the first day of summer. For the Celts, this was as *Beltane*, the beginning of a year's emergence into life. In central Europe, it was the time to move the cattle into the mountain pastures. This was also a day, especially in central and Northern Europe, for the meeting of the Young Men's Society. They would march through the village carrying newly sprouted tree limbs to start a celebration of merrymaking and bonfires.

Moveable – Easter

The traditions associated with May Day often became blurred and adapted to Easter. The importance of Easter increases as one travels east in Europe. Because this holiday is wrapped up in a Church-based celebration, it is difficult to distinguish the folk element from the liturgical.

Summer:

June 24, St. John's Day – Midsummer's Day

In colder parts of Central and Northern Europe, Midsummer's day serves as the time to move the cattle to the mountain pastures (as opposed to May Day when this occurred in warmer climates). Similar practices were consequently associated with St. John's Day in those places. Many regarded the evening preceding Midsummer's Day as a time when spirits could freely roam the world. It was an important night for magic.

Autumn:

September 29. St. Michael's Day

The day before the traditional beginning of autumn (September 30) was a time to celebrate the bounties of harvest. Before the adoption of Christianity, this seems to have been an occasion when various societal rules were cast aside and people's conduct diverted from the acceptable norm. The Church could not tolerate such licentious behavior and so it imposed St. Michael, the warrior angel, as the guardian over the day.

European peasants easily adopted St. Michael as a celestial hero, and the Church managed to alter the pagan holiday into a more innocent celebration of the bounties of the earth.

November 1 and 2. All Saints' Day and All Souls' Day

Of all the holidays of the American calendar, Halloween has perhaps the most ancient roots. Its origins go back to a pagan autumn celebration popular in some parts of Western Europe long before the Christian era. Many prehistoric Europeans regarded November 1 as a time to remember the dead. Finding it impossible to discourage this innocent devotion, the early popes decided to give a Christian veneer to the pagan holiday. The feast of the dead became a mass for all the saints, known in an earlier form of English as "All Hallows' Mass."

The night before was "All Hallows' Eve," a name shortened to Halloween. Priests successfully directed the folk to Christian endeavors during the day of November 1, but the preceding night remained the domain of the wild pagan imagination. People believed that on Halloween, when the sun set, the gate separating this world from the next opened and the dead walked among the living.

The withering vegetation of autumn must have impressed ancient Europeans. Dependent on what food the land had to offer, they saw this as a terrifying event. The death of the world would mean their starvation, and so this became a time to petition the dead for help. People believed that their ancestors could sway the forces of nature to ensure the return of life the next spring.

This is reminiscent of the Christian practice of praying to the saints on November 1 to encourage them to intercede with God on behalf of the living. Long before conversion to Christianity, many Europeans had ritual celebrations intended to influence the dead. For the Romans, it was November 8, and for the Celts, it was November 1. The Irish still retain the ancient term, *Samhain* (pronounced sa-win) for this holiday.

With or without the Christian veneer, this was a time when anything could happen. People believed that witches gathered to make special magic that could only be brewed during the death festival. It was also the night when all sorts of supernatural beings besides the dead were afoot. Demons and imps traveled the land. In Britain, one of the most famous of these was Will-'o-the-Wisp, also known as Jack-'o-Lantern. This entity would lure people into swamps with a dimly-lit torch mimicking the distant light of a farmhouse.

Many different legends account for Will-'o-the-Wisp. Some said that it was the spirit of a man who could not rest because of a wrong committed during life. Others said that it was the spirit of a clever but evil man named

Will or Jack. After death, Will's soul went to heaven where St. Peter recounted the evil deeds of his life. St. Peter refused him entry into heaven and ordered him to hell. Will walked to hell, where he tricked the devil into a bag and beat him or in some other way made the devil fear him. The devil consequently ordered him out of hell. Will's exile condemned him to walk the earth, unwelcome in both heaven and hell. Before he left hell, however, Will stole a piece of burning coal, thinking it would keep him warm. This is the flickering ember that distracts lost travelers, inspiring the carved glowing pumpkin – it was originally a carved turnip in Britain – with a hideous face.

The idea of the Jack-'o-Lantern comes from English and Irish tradition. In fact, it is from the Celts that America inherits most of its notions of what Halloween is supposed to be. Today, the Irish continue the prehistoric traditions of lighting bonfires on Halloween, a practice that many American campuses have translated into homecoming week in autumn. In England, this serves as a root of the November 5 Guy Fawkes celebration, with its bonfires.

The American practice of trick-or-treat derives from the belief that Halloween was a time when spirits walked the earth, but there were other motifs that played into this custom. In the Celtic countries of Western Europe, it was once common to make sacrifices to the dead, leaving food at graves. Some even set the table before retiring for the night so that the visiting dead could enjoy a midnight feast. In turn, the dead were said to leave presents for children. In Christmas-like fashion, youngsters found gifts the following morning.

It was also customary for people to make candy for the dead. Eventually, bakers created elaborate sugar statues depicting Death marching its macabre harvest of corpses and skeletons to the grave. This practice has reached its most elaborate development in Mexico with the celebration of the Day of the Dead.

November 11. St. Martin's Day

St. Martin's Day was the first day of winter in Central and Western Europe. It was the time to slaughter animals and to pay tithes to the Church. A feast of roast goose was customary as part of the bounty provided by culling the stock of animals. A story associating St. Martin with geese reinforced this tradition. According to legend, Martin was a simple, devout resident of Tours, France. The local people elected him as bishop on November 11, but Martin hid in a goose pen, wanting nothing of the honor. When the people of Tours came near, the geese started cackling, and the people found their saintly leader. He ordered, consequently, that geese should pay with their heads on the anniversary of their noisy crime. In fact, a man named Martin, the Bishop of Tours, apparently died on November 11, 397. The legend worked backwards to explain an already existing tradition that had people eating geese on or near that day.

December 6. St. Nicholas' Day

St. Nicholas' Day is one of Europe's most popular winter holidays. Little is known of the historic Nicholas, a figure who is more legendary than real. According to tradition, he died on December 6, 326. Throughout most of the medieval period, people regarded him as one of their favorite saints. He was the spiritual patron of Russia and of mariners, serving sailors as their last hope in times of desperate need. His cult was first popular in the east and then spread to Western Europe in the tenth century.

Nicholas became associated with children when someone playing his part arrived with gifts on December 6. He often appeared riding on a white horse. In some areas, Nicholas was accompanied by his counterpart, known variously as Zwarte Piet, Krampus, or by other names. This was a grimy character who punished lazy, naughty children.

Winter:

December 25 – January 6. The Twelve Nights

The modern celebration of Christmas draws on two European traditions, the pre-Christian, Germanic death festival and the Roman Saturnalia. For the Romans, the shortest days of the year were made even more sacred as the time of the birth of Mithra, a semi-divine figure in a popular mystery cult. Mithra was the son of heaven who descended into the depths of hell to defeat the author of evil in the world. Romans celebrated Mithra's birthday on December 25. The Empire imported and modified the worship of Mithra from the east, where it originated in modern-day Iran. Mithraism, with its strong strain of Stoicism and duty, was especially popular in the Roman army.

In the year 354, the pope declared December 25 as the birthday of Jesus. It was an attempt to incorporate an important holiday and to obscure the worship of a pre-Christian god. When this tradition came north, either in its pre-Christian or Christian form, it met the Germanic death festival. This was a time when the souls of the dead could come back and visit the living, and it was an opportunity to foresee how life would be in the following year.

The ancient idea that Yule is the time for predicting the future is behind the notion of the song "The Twelve Days of Christmas." Modern Americans often misunderstand the twelve days of Christmas, frequently regarding them as the last shopping days before the holiday. In fact, they are the days that begin with Christmas and end on January 6, Epiphany. According to tradition, this was the period that spanned the birth of Jesus and the adoration of the Magi. In America, the twelve days have shifted from a time of celebration to one of preparation. Christmas Day serves as the climax rather than the beginning. Even the wise men now appear on Christmas Eve in most American traditions.

The song "The Twelve Days of Christmas" has meaning now lost to most people. For example, the number of gifts the song describes is no accident. There is, of course, only one gift – the partridge in a pear tree – on the first day, but as anyone knows who has sung the song, the number of gifts quickly escalates. Thus, there are three gifts on the second day – two turtledoves and yet another partridge. There are six gifts on the third day and so forth until seventy-eight gifts appear on the twelfth day. The gifts from all the days total 364, one for each day of the year (minus one).

This is more than a clever trick placed subtly in the carol. European folk culture traditionally viewed the twelve days of Christmas as the time when one could predict the future. Each day represents one of the months of the coming year. By watching the weather or performing magic on any given day, one could forecast the nature of the corresponding month in the following year. The number of gifts in "The Twelve Days of Christmas" apparently draws on the belief that the Christmas season magically reflects the following year.

Yet another tradition surrounding this carol is the role it once occupied as a game. As an Irish farmer from County Clare told a folktale collector in 1940, one child hands another a bucket of turf asking "What's that?" The recipient then answers, "Two ducks and a fat hen," passing it back with the same question, which is answered with an additional three items. The first one to fail reciting the items in order loses. This sort of game appears to be behind the carol "The Twelve Days of Christmas," which retains a humorous quality.

More importantly, however, the song reflects the predictive potential of the season. It was easy for European peasants to assume that the end of one year was a good time to look into the next. By sitting at the crossroads on the night before Christmas and not talking or eating, Icelanders believed that visions of the future would appear.

Many Northern Europeans maintained that a young girl could use magic on Christmas Eve to divine the features of her future husband. With a lighted candle in hand, she could look into the Christmas beer and see his face. By pouring molten lead into water and examining its form, she could predict his occupation – a nail for a carpenter, a horseshoe for a blacksmith, etc.

The American celebration of New Year's Eve includes making noise with horns and shouts as the clock strikes twelve. It is a custom based on European traditions with deep roots. The time of year when the day is at its shortest, when the sun ascends to its lowest point in the sky, was of great importance to European peasants. The winter solstice was the turning point in the peasant calendar, the time when the sun promised to return so that life would renew and crops would be planted. It is not surprising that this time of year attracted superstitions and beliefs, many of which are echoed in today's New Year celebration. In fact, many of these beliefs seem to be prehistoric.

As stated above, this was the time when the Romans celebrated their Saturnalia, a holiday eventually associated with Mithra. The god Janus (hence January) was the obvious Roman patron of the beginning of the year, having as he did two faces, one looking forward and the other looking backward. Janus was also the deity who protected doorways, and stone sculptures of his two-faced image frequently guarded the entrance to a house.

In one of its more important functions, the Saturnalia was a time to remember dead ancestors. With the sun low, supplying so little warmth, Romans as well as many other Europeans seemed to have been reminded of death. Although the Romans like the Celts had a memorial day in early November, the Saturnalia served this purpose as well.

Other people have also focused on the winter solstice as a time to remember the dead. The Germanic cultures regarded this as the most important time to honor departed ancestors, and their pre-Christian traditions have contributed to the holiday celebrations. On the night of the winter solstice (and on December 31 after the introduction of the Julian calendar), peasants lit a candle at the window to guide dead ancestors back home. They then set a meal at the table and placed a large log on the fire, all for the comfort of the uncanny visitors. After doing this, they hurried to bed since they believed seeing the dead could be fatal for the living. These traditions are behind the Christmas candle, the food left for Santa Claus, and the Yule log, but originally, they were associated with the New Year's festival.

Scholars and other enthusiasts have recently paid a great deal of attention to the astronomical significance of Stonehenge, the great prehistoric circle of Britain. Similar stone rings and alignments are scattered throughout Northern Europe. Research has shown that many of these ancient calculators can signal the exact time of the winter solstice. The ability to predict the arrival of the seasons is important for anyone who farms. Knowing the timing of the winter solstice appears to have had religious importance for the builders of European monuments like Stonehenge.

One of the most impressive Irish counterparts to Stonehenge is the burial mound at New Grange. Although the restoration has been criticized by some, this stone-age tomb is well preserved. Tourists can walk into its interior to see engravings and dry-stone masonry, all thousands of years old. For three days around the winter solstice, the rising sun shines through the passage into the burial chamber for seventeen minutes. It is the only time of the year when sunlight reaches the core of New Grange. The builders apparently had designed the mound so that at the crucial time when the dead walked and were remembered, the sun would warm their bodies. Perhaps the builders of the mound saw the breath of sunlight as serving to signal the dead that the time had arrived for their annual foray among the living. In addition, knowing the exact time of the winter solstice was necessary because rituals needed to be performed and precautions taken. After all, one would not want to be wrong and accidentally see dead people walking through the door.

Figure 4. A large megalithic-era carved rock guards the entrance to the tomb at New Grange, Ireland. Neolithic craftsmen carved spirals into its surface to recall the eternal aspect of the universe. The transom above the entrance is positioned so that light enters the burial chamber deep within only once a year.

With the introduction of Christianity and the Julian calendar, England, Scandinavia, and Germany shifted their death festival to January 1, the beginning of the calendar year. Despite Christianity, the death festival and the stories surrounding it survived until recently. In Iceland, for example, it was believed that elves (often sharing many of the attributes of the dead), must find a new home on New Year's Eve. Legends describe people who waited that night on paths the elves would take. If one could remain quiet and still, the elves could not pass and would be forced to grant a gift. Invariably, these intrepid people spoke too soon. The punishment that the vindictive elves gave was insanity or death.

There are many stories about frightful spirits afoot at the end of the year. People believed that with one year ending and the next beginning, a door opened through which the supernatural could pass freely into the natural world. When European ancestral feasts fell into disuse, people still remembered the danger of that night. Most thought it was wise to stay inside, making noise to scare away the demons – the direct ancestors of the New Year's Eve noisemakers.

North America acquired both death festivals, the Celtic one at the beginning of November and the Germanic one at the winter solstice, making its calendar twice as rich. In most cases, however, the folklore as it survives today is a shadow of its former self, with a few American traditions added to a pale survivor of the Old World. In the case of Santa Claus, North America has taken those remnants and created a new tradition worthy of its predecessor. And the strength of that tradition is evidenced in the way it has been successfully exported back to Europe.

America's image of Santa Claus draws on traditions that are thousands of years old. Besides his association with Nicholas, the Christian saint, he is also part elf and part European trickster. Nearly all the world's cultures have the idea that night is the time when the supernatural entities are afoot. As the year turns toward winter and the night grows longer, the supernatural becomes even more at home. As stated above, the winter solstice accentuated this belief.

Scandinavians believed that the household spirit appeared at this time to warm himself by the fire. Called *nisse*, *tomte*, or *gnome*, these supernatural beings could act in good or dangerous ways, depending on their mood or on the nature of the people they confronted. In their little red coats, they guarded the house in a manner that they believed fit the inhabitants. Leave a saucer of milk for such a spirit and all might go well. But woe to the farmer who mocked the *nisse* or who neglected to feed him. An attempt to spy on the *nisse* as he went about his work was also unpardonable. A house's good fortune could shift suddenly with the slightest transgression.

There are many Scandinavian legends describing an innocent child who happened upon the Christmas visit of the *nisse*. The good behavior of a child was rewarded, but the older sister is envious. The following year, the older child intentionally spies upon the spirit. The girl is punished with terrible pain, broken limbs, an ugly face, bad luck, or even death.

The Scandinavian traditions surrounding the Christmas *nisse* parallel the practices of setting out food for Santa Claus. As any child knows, it is strictly forbidden to look at the jolly elf. Even Santa Claus's association with the color red and with the chimney echoes the *nisse's* traditional clothing and his attraction to the hearth. There is, of course, a dramatic shift in the folklore surrounding the *nisse*. On the one hand, there is a serious legend, intended to instruct the listener concerning proper behavior in the face of the supernatural, while its counterpart is a fict, a story told to children, but not believed by the adults.

The American tradition of Santa Claus also has roots in a more malevolent pre-Christian character. The northern European trickster, called "*niccor*" or "Nick," occasionally appeared in the form of a horse that waited for audacious children to climb on his back. The *niccor* then leapt into a lake and drowned his riders. Other stories from throughout Europe have Nick abducting bad children. It is a tradition that is probably behind the story of the Pied Piper of Hamlin, who led children away as punishment for not being paid after ridding the town of rats.

The *niccor* was an important part of pre-Christian folklore in Northern Europe. It was a frightfully powerful entity who inhabited streams and lakes. People made sacrifices to the local *niccor* well into the seventeenth century, long after conversion. With the adoption of Christianity, however, aspects of the trickster blended with the tradition of the *niccor*, confusing it with the devil. Not surprisingly, people often referred to the devil as Old Nick.

Christian monks who converted Northern Europe tried to classify the entire universe into good and evil realms. The *niccor* became officially taboo for Christians, but some could not part with their traditions easily. This was clear to early priests who incorporated pre-Christian traditions and celebrations into the Christian faith and calendar, as stated above. The people of Europe did not want Old Nick banished to hell forever. They told folktales, which characterized the Devil as the trickster, mischievous and occasionally foolish, and he played this role at least as often as that of the evil tormentor of wicked souls.

Still, European peasants were not satisfied with their beloved nature spirit becoming a foolish devil. Before the monks came along, the *niccor* could be good or bad. In the Christian cosmology, he had to be relegated to the dark world only, and so the peasantry created Old Nick's mirror image in the good realm. Jolly Saint Nick, or Santa Claus was born out of this process. After adding a few traits borrowed from the Christmas elf, America of the nineteenth century – but especially after World War II – was ready to take the tradition to its logical extreme as an icon of the premier holiday dedicated to consumerism, the national passion.

Chapter 5 Special Places and Times of Life

For pre-industrial people, several types of places had importance. The house, and especially the fireplace, possessed significance. Many cultures regard the hearth as the spiritual center of the house. Typically, European peasants brought newborn babies and calves to the hearth to make them "house-bound." Recently-hired servants ate their first meal at the fireplace to gain favor for their ensuing occupation.

The doorway or threshold also represented an important part of the dwelling. To protect the human space inside from the supernatural potential outside, people put protective symbols around the door. Because of the significance of iron as a prophylactic against the supernatural, placing iron about the door was a means to protect those within. The idea of hanging a horseshoe above the doorway was part of this tradition, and this practice is still honored by some in Europe and North America.

It was once regarded as advantageous to make a foundation sacrifice of a dog, rooster, or snake buried beneath the doorway so that the spirit of the animal would act as a supernatural guardian of the household. Occasionally a boot or shoe was buried there or near the chimney or elsewhere in the foundation as a surrogate for a person, so that something of the entity that might inhabit the footwear would protect the house. African Americans sometimes buried altered coins in the foundation to convey good fortune to the building and its inhabitants.

Crossroads were also important in European folklore, particularly when the roads crossed at right angles. Such a place had considerable potential for magic and divination because it seemed to refer to the power inherent in a cross. This is apparently an old tradition. Iron Age burial mounds often coincide with crossroads. Ancient Greeks sacrificed animals at crossroads. In more recent times, crossroads were places where witchcraft should be learned, or where it might be possible to call up the Devil to learn a musical skill. Noted African American blues singer, Robert Johnson (1911-1938) was reputed to have acquired his talent from the devil at a crossroad, a story codified in a song called "Cross Road Blues," which has been subsequently covered by numerous musicians, usually using the title "Crossroads."

Water always attracts attention, and internationally, people have tended to see supernatural power in noteworthy places such as springs, wells, waterfalls, deep pools, or remarkable parts of a river. There is archaeological evidence of prehistoric Europeans leaving items in wells and natural springs, apparently with the hope of gaining better health or generally favorable influences from the supernatural. The location of early Christian churches and shrines at wells and springs is evidence of the adaptation of local pagan sacred sites.

Before industrialization, Europeans regarded certain bodies of water either as entities in themselves or as the abodes of supernatural beings. In some cases, it appears that they required sacrifices. The idea that the water being appeared as a horse is widespread throughout Indo-European language areas. But there is a similar tradition in China. In Germanic cultures, this creature is known as the *niccor* or *nicker*. Its association with Odin is underscored by the fact that the Norse god rode Sleipnir, the magical eight-legged horse. Until the sixteenth century, Scandinavian peasants frequently made sacrifices to Odin at pools in the forest. Similarly, the Greek god Poseidon was associated with water, and he rode a chariot drawn by sea horses. Recently-collected folk traditions from Northern Europe depict the *niccor* as an old man playing a violin. There are numerous legends describing ambitious musicians who learned from this supernatural being near his watery abode, or as mentioned previously, at crossroads.

Because of their nature, Churches and chapels were imbued with supernatural power, but the folk often took this in directions not sanctioned by priests. People seeking to divine the future or to practice magic often used a church or chapel as a setting for these non-Christian arts. Similarly, objects taken from the cemetery in a churchyard could have obvious magical potential.

The Progress of Life

People generally divide human life into the stages of childhood, unmarried youth, marriage, and death. Each period required its own set of precautions and practices. More or less formal rites of passage between the stages celebrate the changes and are intended to ensure supernatural grace for an uneventful transition. Besides the divisions by age, groupings by gender are also prevalent, and there are often gender-specific means to celebrate the transition from one period of life to the next.

Pregnancy and childbirth not surprisingly attracted a great deal of attention among the folk. Different cultures have placed a wide variety of taboos on pregnant women. In addition, many European peasants believed that events during each week of pregnancy could foretell and influence the life of the child during the corresponding year of its life. Should a person's mother ignore a taboo at one point, then the child would likely suffer during the annual equivalent. Emancipation from this supernatural burden did not occur until after the age of forty when the effects of the forty weeks of pregnancy came to an end.

Taboos during pregnancy included a prohibition against a pregnant woman sitting in a chair fastened with nails, since with a violation, the child will suffer from skin disease. If the woman were to witness an accidental fire, the child would have a fever. A pregnant woman who watched an execution or the slaughtering of animals might cause her child to have leprosy or convulsions. If she saw the head of a rabbit, the child might be hare-lipped, a concern that inspired hunters to bring rabbits to market without heads.

Extensive taboos and actions were needed in the minds of the European peasant to ensure a problem-free birth and to protect the well-being of mother and infant. During labor, locks needed to be unlocked, knots untied, and peas boiled, all to reverse the effect that such objects might have in restricting the birth canal.

One common practice related to childbirth resulted in a traditional fict of western culture. A woman was in jeopardy during birth because a host of supernatural creatures might attempt to abduct her and leave a replica in her place that would appear to be her corpse. To avoid such a fate, people ushered children outside and sealed the house. When the birth was complete, the doors and windows could be reopened and the children returned. There was a need, however, to explain the arrival of the infant.

Parents wanting to avoid the topic of conception and childbirth relied on the fact that the only opening to the house was the chimney. Coincidentally, European peasants had observed that storks nested on the little-used gallows or "Catherine" wheel in towns. These looked like wagon wheels positioned horizontally on tall poles, and storks found them a safe place to nest. The birds were regarded as good luck, so it was not uncommon for people to construct a similar wheel on top of their roofs to attract storks. When children asked about the origin of the infant, it was easy to suggest that it had arrived by way of the chimney and that the stork had accomplished this deed.

The extraordinary nature of childbirth required sanctification of mother and infant, and until this was accomplished, both needed special magical attention. The family would hang an axe or knife over the doorway and above the crib because the offending supernatural beings would avoid both iron and sharp objects. The fire was kept burning day and night, and the baby's bath water needed to be thrown to the east or south, since the other two directions would bring negative results.

There are indications that before conversion to Christianity, Germanic cultures required mother and child to be sprinkled with water to reintroduce them into society. After conversion, this practice was easily modified into the baptism of the infant. The mother still needed special attention, but second baptisms were against Church policy. There was, consequently, a ceremony called "churching," which readmitted the mother as a member of the community.

Until adolescence, children needed protection from supernatural beings who regarded them as good targets for abduction. The young were frequently dressed in the protective color red. Supernatural beings treasured small boys, in part a reflection of the value that peasants placed on boys as sources of agricultural labor, but this also responded to the demographic fact that more young boys die of childhood diseases than girls. Because of this, parents often dressed male infants as girls to make them less desirable.

There was a great deal of attention paid to one's entry into adolescence. Rituals included admission into a young person's society, but these were almost always reserved for adolescent boys. Young women were strictly regulated by the "goose walk," older women who took care to limit their promiscuity. After losing one's virginity, a woman's hair gained supernatural potency that could affect crops. The hair of women should be bound, consequently, especially when near farmland or entering a church. Aprons were also designed to protect food while being prepared, and this garment needed to be worn when attending church since the pubic region of a woman carried with it a degree of supernatural potential. By regularly inspecting adolescent girls, groups of older women in a village could publicly declare the loss of virginity by forcing a young woman to suddenly take on the scarf and apron, leaving little question that the adolescent in question was no longer a virgin. The possibility of this public shaming inhibited pre-martial sexual activity.

Marriage conferred full membership into society. The idea of matrimonial gifts exchanged between the couple was common. The groom frequently gave the bride an ornately carved wooden spoon. The bride often gave the man a set of clothes.

Ceremonies associated with death were perhaps most endowed with ritual and magical practices. Death was an opportunity to ensure the eternal well-being of a friend or relative. It could also provide the living with a powerful supernatural ally. Burial practices in Western Europe generally reflect positive attitudes toward the dead. The farther to the east in Europe one looks, one finds cultures increasingly concerned with the possibility of the dead walking after death. People regarded the deceased as malevolent and dangerous. These generalizations can be easily challenged by contrary examples from various regions; the diversity of humanity is key even though there are regional trends.

There is archaeological evidence of feelings toward the dead. In Western Europe, Neolithic societies buried the deceased in collective mounds where the bones accumulated. People made seasonal gifts at the entrances to these chambers apparently to procure continued good will from the otherworld and to ensure that departed loved ones would have a comfortable existence. In the east, prehistoric burials were typically solitary. It is not uncommon to find remains that were tightly bound in a fetal position. Individuals who seem to have inspired the most concern had rocks shoved into their mouths and large stones placed above their burials. These were apparently intended to keep the dead from talking and from walking from the grave. This sort of archaeological evidence can also be found in burials from historic periods. Again, any effort to see these contrasting traditions as rigidly defined by geography is called to question by exceptions.

The Eastern European tradition of the walking dead has diffused into North America thanks to the literary and cinematic use of the *Nosferatu*, the vampire. That said, the idea of walking corpses cannot be regarded as entirely an eastern phenomenon: the animated dead also played an important role in medieval Icelandic sagas. Here, the *aptrganga maður* – the "after walking man" – was especially troublesome and required the bravery and strength of a great hero to end its reign of terror. Chopping off the head of the corpse and placing it between the body's legs was one of the only ways to put these monsters to rest.

Throughout European peasant society, there was also a great deal of concern about determining when a person had "passed over." In modern times, it may seem obvious that death occurs when the heart stops. Even today, however, the line between life and death can be vague, occasionally requiring a judicially-determined definition. And even this can become the subject of political squabbling. In the modern world, death can be defined as brain-dead, but then there can be a question about whether it is appropriate, ethical, or legal to "pull the plug" to stop the heart from beating when the brain ceases to function. In traditional European society, the line between life and death was far more ambiguous. A person still living by today's standards could cross over into the domain of death because of a disease, immense old age, or because of a curse. A large catch of fish or some other extraordinary circumstance might also signal the transition even when dealing with a healthy, young person.

In the Icelandic sagas, these people were *feigr*, or "fated to die." This is echoed in the archaic English word "fey" as in "he had a fey look about him." In other words, the person was destined to die, and somehow the shadow of death had already descended over him even though his heart continued to beat. A person who had made this transition withdrew from normal society and activities, preparing to die. Society regarded the person as essentially dead.

In the same way, the dead could do almost as much as the living. Medieval stories tell of the dead walking, talking, eating, and having sex. Obviously, such occurrences were to be feared and there were many rituals and forms of magic intended to keep the dead in the peaceful quiet of eternal sleep. In contrast, there was also a wide variety of magical practices available for the brave few who would call upon the dead to do their bidding.

European folklore includes the idea that the time of death was predetermined. There was a general feeling that a certain number of tasks or obligations must be completed before a person could die. Those who had committed suicide were forced to walk the earth as ghosts until the appointed time of their natural death. In addition, the place of burial was predestined. North American culture preserves the older European tradition of interpreting a sudden shiver as evidence that someone has just walked over one's final resting place – a location that is as predetermined as the time of death.

People regarded a wide variety of events as foretelling death. A death would occur in a family if the Christmas candle went out, if the door opened by itself, if a clock stopped, if a bird flew into the house, or if a fox came near the door.

Death in the family required a constant vigil so the dead would have company. In many cultures, coins would be placed on the eyes to keep them from opening, something that can happen naturally with a corpse. Tradition required that candles burn constantly. In Eastern Europe, people believed that the dead soul continued to walk the earth for forty days, after which it could ascend or descend to its respective destiny. There was, consequently, a second funeral forty days after death.

Chapter 6 Divination and Witchcraft

Liljeblad defined divination "as the art of determining the unknown by supernatural means, whether this concerns future events or occurrences, which are distinct in space." He further identifies three ways that such knowledge could be obtained: 1. A gifted person acquires knowledge through ecstasy, a spiritual moment of insight; 2. Dreams or visions can also grant knowledge about the future or of far off places; and finally, 3. Through training or gifted insight, a person is able to read natural occurrences as indicative of the future or distant events.

Ecstatic or shamanistic divination: With this means of divination, someone intentionally brings on a trance to communicate with the supernatural world. The shaman typically deals with a friendly spirit who may be a guardian, or a spirit speaks through the shaman. Many arctic people such as the Lapps, the Tungus, the Mongols, the Inuit, and some American Indians, maintain the tradition of a spirit speaking through a shaman by means of ecstasy. Icelandic sagas describe this approach to divination, always attributing the skill to women. This sort of divination did not survive Christianization in Europe.

Dreams and Visions: Before industrialization, Europeans commonly practiced divination through acquired visions and dreams. Someone wanting a vision would avoid eating and talking to separate themselves from the human world. The person would then go to places such as crossroads or cemeteries the night before an important holiday, for a chance to communicate with the supernatural world. People also stared into a shiny object – a crystal, a lustrous stone, a mirror, a polished piece of metal, or a liquid – until they saw visions. Those who claimed special skills or gifts to predict the future with these means occasionally practiced divination as a profession. Often, however, vision seeking was the domain of non-professionals who simply wished to gain insight into the future or distant events. For example, an unmarried girl in Scandinavia would peer into the newly-brewed Christmas beer with a lighted candle to see her future husband.

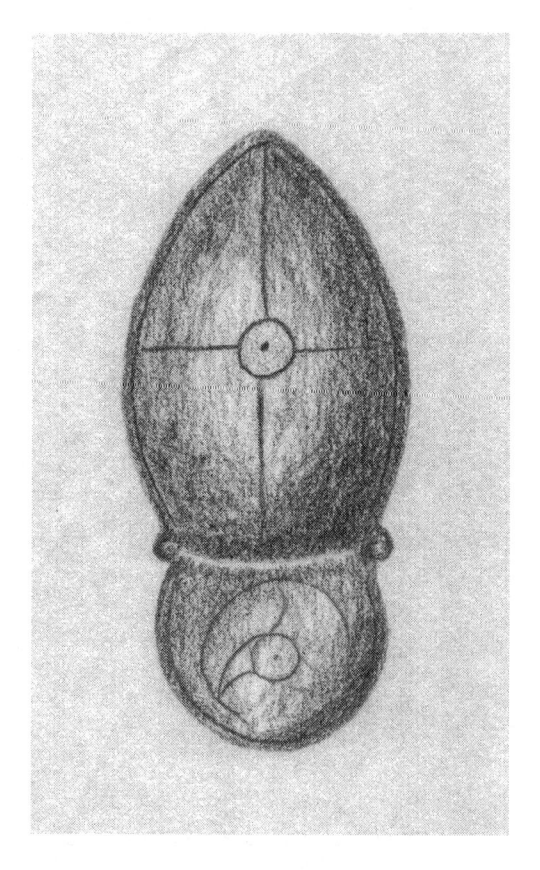

Figure 5. First Century, CE, Irish divination spoon. It appears to draw on the power of the four directions of the world. Quadrants were probably used to predict the future or to divine other truths. National Museum of Ireland, Dublin.

European peasants also regarded dreams as important elements of divination. Elaborate means to interpret dreams are characteristic of folklore and have been one of the most resilient forms of tradition in the face of industrialization and the post-modern world.

Interpretation of natural events: Many people regard various natural phenomena as indicators of future events. The flight of birds, the internal organs of animals, the appearance of the new moon at the beginning of a season, the movement of smoke from a fire, or any number of other things could be used to predict the future. The Roman science of augury took this form of divination to an extreme, but the folk have always sought signs from nature to indicate the future.

Interpretations of events in the world are often opportunistic in that someone divining the future may see significance in odd occurrences, without any specific significance identified in the local folklore. Other subjects of divination are clearly defined by oral tradition. The Irish and some places in Britain, for example, regard the number of magpies first seen in the morning as an indication of how the day will proceed. The Irish have a rhyme, which has been recorded with several variations, that recites the possibilities: "one for sorrow, two for joy," and so on for indications of everything from luck to poor business dealings.

Cornish-born historian A. L. Rowse (1903-1997) recorded the rhyme as "one for sorrow, two for mirth; three for a wedding, four for a birth." The selection of the magpie for this special role is no accident. The name magpie was originally "Morgana's Pie," a reference to the powerful female deity who was the basis of the Arthurian character Morgan le Fey. The magpie was a sacred bird for the goddess, and so its appearance in a variety of numbers could originally be taken as a predication of the future from the goddess. The Irish have forgotten the pagan associations of the magpie as a means of divining the future. Nevertheless, they turn to the bird, a choice with deep roots in folklore.

Witchcraft: Throughout European history, there have been examples of people who specialized in the use of the magical arts. In general, these people followed the craft for the benefit of others within a village. Anti-social witchcraft is rare in historical records, and those practicing magic to the benefit of the community were often highly regarded.

During the medieval period, witches continued to practice their craft, but the Church steadily escalated its interest in and opposition to their activities. Still, the idea that witches were evil did not become widespread until the fifteenth century. Several factors caused this change, not the least of which was the Church's attempt to root out pagan survivals. Not surprisingly, the Church classified holdovers of the old religion as evil, a concept that European peasants were slow to grasp.

A crisis occurred in peasant society during the late medieval period as pressure from the aristocracy and the land-holding Church caused a shift away from dairy culture to farms producing grains. Well into prehistory, European peasants regarded cattle as a source of wealth. The English word "fee" comes from the Anglo-Saxon word for cattle. The same is true for the

Latin root of "pecuniary." The problem with a dairy culture, however, is that it is extremely difficult to tax. Grain production allows for the amassing of agricultural wealth, and so the Church and the aristocracy increasingly forced peasants to grow more grains at the expense of their pastures and cattle.

European peasants consequently faced a shrinking pool of wealth. Put more plainly, their herds were dwindling. At the same time, the Church was condemning magical practices as evidence of pacts with the devil. Peasants, increasingly anxious about declining wealth, began to look to practitioners of magic as the evil source of their economic demise. Although there are earlier examples of trials, reputed witches found themselves condemned in larger numbers beginning in the 1480s.

Of course, historians have considered the question of what caused the witch craze, and in the process, they have identified many factors that certainly contributed to the hysteria. Finding a cause for the witch craze is a complex problem, and it is probably better to discuss multiple, complementary causes and influences. Regardless of the origin of this phenomena, the primary documents associated with the prosecution of witches provide an opportunity to peer into late medieval folklore.

The election of Pope Innocent VIII in 1484 added another dimension to the situation when he issued a formal statement against witchcraft. He further commissioned Heinrich Kramer (ca. 1430-1505) to research and write a book documenting the perceived epidemic of witchcraft. The author included the respected name of Jakob Sprenger (ca. 1436-1495) as a co-author of the resulting publication, but the extent of the learned academic's participation in the project is not clear. The resulting *Malleus Maleficarum (The Witches' Hammer)* appeared in 1487. Because its publication occurred shortly after the invention of the Gutenberg Press, the book received wide dissemination, and it became a sensation, appearing in twenty-nine printings by 1669.

The *Malleus Maleficarum* remains one of the most useful documents portraying medieval beliefs about the subject. But because of its popularity, the publication not only documented current folk belief, but it also influenced it. This was the period of the great witch trials. Although Papal authority started the witch craze, it became severe in Protestant countries where economic transitions and resulting strains were common. Thus, almost no witches were executed in Ireland or Italy, and it was relatively rare in France. Most victims lived in Germany, the Scandinavian Countries, and Britain.

The witch trials left a large body of documents that can be regarded as preserving contemporary folklore. Indeed, much of the material reflects an older, pre-Christian layer of medieval folklore as Christian forces sought to discredit and destroy remnants of the old religion. Conversion of the North had been, after all, somewhat superficial, and the folk maintained many older practices. The witch trials provided an excellent opportunity for the Church, whether Roman or Protestant, to label pre-Christian religious practices as evil and then to cause them and their practitioners to be exterminated.

There is diverse evidence of the witch trials, a subject that will remain a fertile subject of research into the foreseeable future. A report in the November/December 2000 issue of *Archaeology* underscores the on-going investigation and discovery associated with the subject. In an excavation in London, archaeologists found what they initially thought was a sixteenth-century wine bottle. Testing, however, revealed that it was in fact a "witch bottle" filled with urine and bent brass pins. People prepared these bottles and buried them beneath houses as prophylactics against witchcraft. A witch practicing magic on people living in a protected house would find the spell reversed and urination as difficult as if she had a bladder full of pins.

Chapter 7 Stories from Ancient Times

Myths and the ancient religions of the world offer opportunities for insight into the folk mind of long ago. As stated in Chapter 1, a myth, if the term is properly used, is a step away from oral tradition. Nonetheless, historical documents can shed a great deal of light on beliefs and stories that have disappeared or changed over time. There are a few general things that can be said about the beliefs and customs of the ancient world based on the imperfect sources that remain.

Ancient people believed in the power of magic. They were also certain that a wide variety of supernatural beings inhabited the world. Legends give evidence that these creatures existed to serve as a guide for behavior and interaction with the spiritual world. In addition, it was not uncommon for ancient people to have some vague concept of an overarching power greater than all the rest. This entity often served as the prime mover of the world, and although it was occasionally regarded as generally disinterested and unapproachable, it could be thought of as a god in the modern sense of the word.

In literate societies, shamans were organized into priesthoods, and leaders were elevated to royalty. Priests invariably attempted to harness the power of local oral traditions to codify the cultural bedrock and belief systems of diverse but related people. It quickly became clear to these early folklore collectors that people from the different regions within the realm told similar stories but with variations that made each distinct. Priests typically provided the standard, definitive source for each of the stories, codifying them into the official state version. Because the illiterate masses have always had profound respect for the written word, the documents elevated these versions of the stories, and often this had the effect of exterminating contradictory elements of oral tradition.

In the process of recording folklore, priests also promoted some supernatural beings to a pantheon of gods and lesser gods. Authors of these early texts usually combined the features of the most powerful male supernatural beings with the vague god-like prime mover. This gave society a heavenly counterpart of the earthly king, and priests used the comparison to elevate the stature of the human ruler. In addition, priests took advantage of the situation by claiming the exclusive ability to intermediate with these gods. Of course, the original supernatural beings were powerful, feared, respected, and often placated with sacrifices and other magical means to win favor. Their transformation to the status of gods could be subtle and there were variations with each society. The important thing to remember is that the recorded myths of ancient cultures were based on folk traditions, but they were transformed to suit specific purposes.

There is evidence that some societies of the ancient world regarded the prime mover as a mother goddess. This has become a politically-charged topic because some modern authors maintain that there have been efforts to obscure the history of the mother goddess to suit the sexist ends of a male-dominated society. According to this idea, there was once a peaceful matriarchal society that worshiped the goddess and grew crops. Warriors from elsewhere arrived and destroyed the paradise, imposing their male god as ruler while displacing women as leaders. The basis for the theory is the Indo-European migrations. It appears that a male-dominated pantheon did migrate into Europe, but the question arises as to whether there was a clear demarcation between a male-centered religion and one that worshipped a goddess exclusively.

The prehistoric Balkans provides feminists with an excellent opportunity to develop the image of a matriarchal society and corresponding pantheon because little is known about the earlier society and it is possible to fill in details as one chooses. The imposition of an imagined matriarchal society on the past does a disservice, however, to what is known about the prehistory of the region. Despite exaggerations, it seems that a mother goddess was indeed extremely important in the Balkans during prehistoric times. She may have influenced the status of women, although a few clay statues of goddesses cannot prove such a conclusion. There is evidence that a warrior society invaded and perhaps conquered the Balkans and the Greek peninsula as early as four millennia ago. The invasion may correspond to the introduction of the Greek language into the area, and it may coincide with the period when a dominant male god took over the pantheon, although none of this can be said with certainty. Legends recorded during the Classical Greek period give us the best clues as to what may have occurred, but everything is speculative.

Figure 6. Síleagh-na-gig (Sheila of the Beasts) was an ancient birthing goddess who appears in stonework throughout Ireland and Britain. This is from the twelfth-century Kilpeck Church near Hereford, England.

Greek myths reveal ambivalence between the gods and goddesses and their relative status. Hera was clearly a powerful goddess, and it appears that she, together with Aphrodite and Athena, may represent an older prehistoric layer of belief and culture when the goddess was dominant. It even appears that the goddess may have taken the form of a trinity, the mother, lover, and wise woman as three manifestations of the same entity. The struggles of Zeus, Poseidon, and Ares against these powerful goddesses may echo cultural clashes of centuries earlier. There is, however, a limit to how far this can be taken with credibility.

The powerful role various prehistoric mother goddesses may have played is made more apparent by more recent religious manifestations. Corresponding to the ancestor of Hera and her cohort is the Middle Eastern goddess Isis/Ishtar. There can be little question that these were powerful supernatural forces in the minds of believers, but the effect of the entities was not restricted to prehistoric or Classical times. The Islamic fascination with Fatima, the daughter of Mohammed, provided the fiercely monotheistic faith with a feminine object of near-religious adoration. Similarly, the cult of the Virgin Mary in medieval Christianity was strongest in areas where the ancient mother goddess was apparently most popular. Although Fatima may have partially inspired the worship of Mary, the Christian devotion certainly draws strength from old indigenous roots.

Greek and Roman Gods

Greek	Roman	Function
Aphrodite	Venus	Love and beauty
Apollo	Apollo	Reason and prophesy
Ares	Mars	War
Artemis	Diana	The hunt
Asclepius	Aesculapius	Healing and medicine
Athena	Minerva	Wisdom
Cronus	Saturn	Father of Zeus/Jupiter
Demeter	Ceres	Agriculture
Dionysus	Bacchus	Wine and frivolity
Eros	Cupid	Love
Hades	Dis/Pluto	Death/the underworld
Heracles	Hercules	Son of Zeus/Jupiter; hero
Hermes	Mercury	Messenger of the gods
Hestia	Vesta	The hearth
Pan	Faunus	Ruler of the forest
Poseidon	Neptune	Oceans and rivers
Tyche	Fortuna	Fate
Zeus	Jupiter	Supreme sky god

Origin and Other Myths

Folklorists and ethnographers have collected hundreds if not thousands of international stories describing the origin of the world, humanity, fire, and various other things. Depending on the circumstance, many of these legends are called myths. They feature supernatural beings of greater or lesser power, which sources generally refer to as gods. Whether the terms "myth" and "god" are appropriate is a matter of debate, but clearly this material represents a remarkable array of diverse traditions.

It would be possible to focus on any one of the world collections of mythology to illustrate the possibilities, but when the term mythology is used in English, it often refers to ancient Greek and Roman traditions. References to Classical mythology permeate European and North American culture. The only collection of mythology that is equally important to European and North American culture comes from the Semitic world in the form of the Old Testament. The influence of the Bible on Europe must not be underestimated, but an overview of Classical mythology can provide a better understanding of how the folk viewed a diverse spiritual world influencing everything from creation to weather patterns.

Like most groups that spoke an Indo-European language, the Greeks and Romans conceived of a pantheon with a dominant male sky god. Myths dealing with the succession of power in divine generations reveals ambiguity concerning who was the supreme deity. The mythology of these people often included a vague concept of a passive, remote father god. Long ago, he set things in motion and then stepped back, leaving specific worldly matters to his squabbling children. In the recorded myths of Greeks, Romans, and the Germanic people, the leading male figure then assumed many of the characteristics and much of the role of this ambiguous all-father. Greek and Roman myth portray the early dominating god as Cronus or Saturn, respectively. In Scandinavian myth, the role of the prime god was often attributed to Týr/Tiw, from which we have the word Tuesday.

The role of the active ruling male god in Greek myth is split. Zeus and Poseidon were fierce rivals. Zeus – a cognate of Latin *Deus*, a word for god, and of the Anglo-Saxon name for the god Tiw – was the powerful god of the sky. In typical Indo-European fashion, he wielded thunderbolts, fought giants, and ruled the divine world. There was also a widespread early male divinity linked to rivers and to horses. This relationship is discussed elsewhere; suffice it to say here that there are historical documents telling of Scandinavian peasants making sacrifices to bodies of water with the hope of currying the favor of the local spirit. Because the supreme god was sometimes linked with water and horses, he often manifested as a water horse. The water god could be part fish and part horse, or he could be thought of as merely a horse that emerged from the water. Poseidon, consequently, rides the waves pulled by a chariot and water horses.

Northern myth has a similar rivalry between two male supernatural beings. Odin (Óðinn in Old Norse), the god of wisdom and magic, rides his magnificent, eight-legged horse Sleipnir. He occasionally appears as the dominant god of the pantheon, and historically, sacrifices could be made to him either in the form of hangings or with victims drowned in pools of water. His Anglo-Saxon counterpart was named Woden, from which we derive the word Wednesday. There was also an all-powerful sky god. Like Zeus and the Roman Jupiter, he threw thunderbolts and fought giants. From his name, Thor, we have the words thunder and Thursday.

Before stories about these entities were written down, the supernatural beings were probably amorphous, occasionally combining and separating. Beliefs recorded in non-literate cultures suggest that supernatural entities frequently exchange characteristics from the point of view of person to person, place to place, and time to time. In the fluid realm of oral tradition, the water-horse god sometimes fused with the sky god. Or perhaps they were one in the same, with two manifestations that occasionally drifted apart. With expressions in many linguistic groups and over millennia, it should come as no surprise that attributes would be shared and personas would merge and diverge numerous times. Untethered by written documents, belief systems can drift in numerous directions, but certain core themes continue to resonate. When authors sought to codify what people believed to be true, they imposed an artificial structure on something that could not be described with precision. And yet once it was recorded, people looked to the document as the ultimate expression – the canon – of the religion.

Classical myth also had a powerful female goddess, and as previously noted, it appears that the significance of the character was tied to the Mediterranean area where there was likely an underlying important mother goddess. She is Hera in Greek myth, and Juno for the Romans. Again, there appears to have been a split of characteristics into separate entities as described by the early writers. Evidence suggests that Aphrodite, the beautiful goddess of love, Athena, the goddess of wisdom, and Hera, the goddess of motherhood, were on occasion regarded as manifestations of the same supernatural being. The problem for subsequent scribes was not unlike that faced by those who worked with the Christian concept of the Trinity, which maintains that the Father, the Son, and the Holy Spirit are three distinct and yet permanently-linked entities. A scribe attempting to address the subtleties of such a concept would need to choose between addressing the Trinity in superficially separate terms and dealing with the entwined nature of the more intricate concept of unity. Classical authors who dealt with their contemporary belief systems dropped the complexity for whatever reason. Northern myth has the goddess Freya, the sister of Frey, who with her brother takes on the role of promoting fertility, but the goddess does not attain the stature of her southern sisters.

A diverse realm of gods and goddesses fill the Classical pantheons of Greece and Rome. In the assortment of supernatural beings there are echoes of stories recorded from separate locations, heroes elevated to the status of gods by scribes, and invented deities that suited the needs of the state at specific moments.

The story of Wayland the Smith illustrates the vague nature of the boundaries between deity, elf, and hero, and between legend and myth. Wayland (also spelled Weyland and Weland) was a fantastic metal worker whose legendary exploits were told throughout pre-Christian Northern

Europe. Unfortunately, most surviving references to him are fragmentary, but they serve as evidence of his widespread popularity and of the cohesive nature of his tale. His story is told most fully in the thirteenth-century poem from Iceland called the "Völundarkviða," from which it is possible to make sense of the briefer references in other literature. There is ambiguity, however, in the Norse sources as to what Wayland, or in this case Völundr, was. One Scandinavian document refers to him as *álfa lioði* and *vísi álfa*, meaning prince or lord of the elves. Still, for the most part, the literature seems to regard him as a man in an extraordinary distant past.

Figure 7. The Anglo-Saxon Franks Casket dates to roughly 700 CE. The front panel depicts the Adoration of the Magi on the right. Runes above the three men spell the word "Magi." The star of Bethlehem is above them as they present their gifts to Jesus and the Virgin Mary. The left part of the panel is dedicated to the pre-Christian story of Wayland the Smith. With hammer and tongs, Wayland has crafted a cup from the skull of a prince, whose headless body rests at the smith's feet. The princess Beadohild accepts a drugged drink from the cup. Wayland or his brother is killing geese to craft magic wings for an escape. The runic inscription around the border is a riddle. It reads, "*Fisc flodu ahof on fergenberig. Warþ gasric grom þær he on greut giswom.*" This translates, "The flood lifted up the fish onto the mountainous cliff. The king of terror became sad when he swam on the shingle." The answer on the left side of the front panel reads, "*hronæs ban*" or "whale bone," the material used to make the little box. The casket is an excellent example of the Anglo-Saxon use of runes as well as the ability of newly-converted European societies to place Christian images next to pagan myth.

The story of the smith begins with his capture by King Nithhad. To ensure that Wayland stays put, the king cuts the hero's hamstrings. In revenge, the smith kills the king's son and fashions a gilded goblet from his skull. He uses this to serve a drugged drink to Beadohild, the king's daughter, whom he then rapes and impregnates. Wayland, with his extraordinary skill as a craftsman, fashions wings from the feathers of geese he has killed and flies away from imprisonment, leaving disaster in his wake as revenge for his ill treatment.

This story is reminiscent of the Greek legend of Daedalus, the extraordinary blacksmith whose exploits included imprisonment on Crete by King Minos. He escaped the island by crafting feathered wings for himself and Icarus, his son. The story of that tragic exploit is well known. Icarus flew too close to the sun, melting the wax that fastened the feathers, and the young man fell to the sea and drowned.

The name Daedalus means "bright" or "cunningly wrought" and there are several motifs that link the hero with Hephaestus, the divine smith of the Greek Pantheon. Robert Graves, an authority on Greek myth, suggested that "Hephaestus" means "he who shines by day." The gods flung Hephaestus from Olympus, and he consequently hobbled as he walked. His Roman counterpart is the lame smith-god Vulcan, a name etymologically related to Wayland/Weland/Völundr. When combining and comparing the various motifs, it appears that there was a widespread story of a remarkable smith who angered a king, was imprisoned and mutilated so he could not walk fast. This hero then fled imprisonment, often by using his skill to craft magic wings.

The variants illustrate how easily a character of a popular story can slide between god, elf, and human hero. It is possible that the various oral traditions, spread over expanses of time and space, were self-contradictory. At the same time, it is important to remember that the authors who recorded these stories may or may not have been true to the oral traditions that they heard. It is simply not possible to sort out where the problem of diversity lies, or even if there is a problem. Oral traditions are notoriously amorphous and finding the definitive version of any story is an elusive goal. There is no "correct" account of a story; there are only numerous manifestations.

Chapter 8 Stories from Pre-Industrial Europe

When the discipline of folklore is not concerned with beliefs and customs, oral tradition is what remains. By this, a folklorist is referring to that aspect of culture conveyed entirely by word of mouth. With an increasingly literate society, new traditions emerge such as Xerox lore and now Internet lore. Before the dramatic turns of the nature of the folk and their media in the late twentieth century, however, folktales, legends, proverbs, riddles, and jokes were expressed almost exclusively with the spoken word.

The Folktale

As stated in the earlier section on definitions, folklorists often use the German term *Märchen* to discuss the folktale. In Russian it is *skazka*. In Danish and Norwegian it is *eventyr*, which means adventure. From India to Ireland, folktales typically rely on supernatural motifs. The folktales from the Semitic world are often more realistic. Europeans borrowed this material, which folklorists label as novella or romantic tales.

The famous Finnish folklorist Antti Aarne (1867-1925) started the herculean task of cataloguing and organizing collected material related to the European folktale as well as other material. He published his first edition in 1910 and issued a second in 1928. The American Stith Thompson took over the project and issued his own edition. The German scholar Hans-Jörg Uther offered yet another expanded edition, this one appearing in 2004. Tale types are expressed with the initials AT followed by a number, but that is now often expressed as ATU. Aarne's beginning point for classification is as follows:

First group: Animal Tales (typically one or two episodes); Type numbers 1-299.

Second Group: Ordinary Folktales (multi-episodic); Type numbers 300-1199 with the following subgroups:

A. Tales of Magic 300-749
   300-399 Supernatural Adversary
   400-459 Supernatural or Enchanted Husband or Wife
   460-499 Supernatural Task
   500-559 Supernatural Helper
   560-649 Magic Object
   650-699 Supernatural Power of Knowledge
   700-749 Other Tales of the Supernatural

B. Religious Tales; Type numbers 750-849

C. Novella (Romantic but Realistic Tales); Type numbers 850-999

D. Tales of the Stupid Ogre; Type numbers 1000-1199

Third Group: Jokes and Anecdotes; Type numbers 1200-1999

Regardless of the edition, the "Tale Type Index" lists all the known tale types recorded in European folklore. It also identifies variants and describes some of the distribution based on recorded and catalogued material. Subsequent indexes have focused on specific countries. The Irish Tale Type Index, for examples, employs the same structure that originated with the work of Aarne. The Japanese index, however, can only refer to the European index in general terms since its oral tradition is distinct from the shared oral tradition that manifested from India to Ireland.

Originally, folklorists hoped to answer questions regarding the origin of oral traditions. Many early scholars – including Jacob Grimm – believed that folktales represented the shattered remains of an ancient religion. By collecting and assembling the pieces, they hoped to reconstruct a prehistoric, Indo-Germanic religion. After more than a century of study, folklorists generally agree to one of two fundamental conclusions regarding this approach. Either the origin of a given folktale type is too illusive to define exactly, or the types are more recent than early folklorists had hoped. Often both conclusions come to play simultaneously, but the net result is that modern folklorists almost always stress different questions in the study of oral traditions.

The preoccupation with origins affected the study of the folktale more than that of legends, largely because the folktale seemed to be the oldest form of oral tradition. Legends had the appearance of being short-lived, given their limited distributions. Folktales, on the other hand, were often international and seemed to refer to an ancient time. Studies that were preoccupied with the origin of a folktale type are useful now for the encyclopedia-like treatment of the material, but some of their conclusions can be discarded.

At the turn of the century, Axel Olrik (1864-1917) at the University of Copenhagen took a different approach. This Danish scholar was influential in the early development of Scandinavian folklore. In 1909, he published his *"Epische Gesetze der Volksdictung"* ("Epic Laws of Folk Narrative"). It was originally presented at a congress of scholars in Berlin in 1908. Other folklorists expanded Olrik's work based on his notes, publishing new editions of the essay in 1919 and in 1921.

The important contributions of Olrik's brief article are twofold. First, he broke from a concern about origins and started looking at other questions concerning the nature of oral tradition. His approach anticipates the structuralists after the war, but unlike those later scholars, he does not deny the validity of the Type as a concept.

Olrik's classic work was made available to the English-speaking world in a translation published in Alan Dundes's reader, *The Study of Folklore* (1965: 129-141). Olrik arrived at more than a dozen laws (the exact number appears differently in various incarnations), which he suggested govern oral tradition. These laws would play a critical role in keeping a type hemmed in so that if a storyteller introduced a deviant variation, the next storyteller would correct it. Olrik's laws are so important that is appropriate to explain them in full:

1. The Law of Opening and the Law of Closing. By this, Olrik meant that a tale begins with a peaceful setting and moves to excitement. It does not abruptly start with the most important motif. As a mirror image of this, the ending starts with excitement and transforms to calm. Olrik pointed out that the longer the tale, the longer the ending needed to be. Shorter narratives could use briefer endings. He further used the example of a folktale not ending with the deaths of the lovers, but rather with the rose bushes growing from the graves, their flowers intertwining.

2. The Law of Repetition. Folk narrative repeats action for emphasis. Olrik pointed out that the hero may go into a field three days in a row to kill giants, or that he tries three times to ride up a glass mountain. In literature, these events would be as different as possible; in folk narrative, they are as similar as possible. Olrik wrote: "every time a striking scene occurs in a narrative, and continuity permits, the scene is repeated."

3. The Law of Three. In Indo-European and Semitic folktales, repetition occurs in threes. This almost has the appearance of being universal, but there are important exceptions. Where there are three repetitions or three

brothers in a European folktale, the story in India will feature four, in keeping with the importance of that number in the subcontinent. Similarly, various American Indian cultures feature four or five as the preferred number, and this manifests in its oral tradition. Olrik made the point that literature, with the need for great realism, has fallen away from this rule, leaving oral tradition as the original form of storytelling exhibiting this rigid approach to narrative.

4. The Law of Two to a Scene. Olrik pointed out that "two is the maximum number of characters who appear at one time. Three people appearing at the same time, each with his own individual identity and role to play, would be a violation of tradition." Olrik went on to discuss the "Law of Two to a Scene" in relation to the story of Siegfried's battle with Frafnir, the dragon. "Throughout, only two characters appear on the stage at one time: Siegfried and Regin, Siegfried and his mother, Siegfried and Odin, Siegfried and Fafnir, Siegfried and the bird, Siegfried and Grani. The Law of Two to a Scene is so rigid that the bird can speak to Siegfried only after Regin has gone to sleep." Olrik also noted that in another folktale the princess must remain silent as the hero battles the dragon who has abducted her.

5. The Law of Contrast. Throughout a tale there will be a series of contrasts. A sad woman is contrasted with a happy one. Olrik used the examples of young and old, large and small, man and monster, good and bad, strong and weak, or for that matter, stupid and wise.

6. The Law of Twins. This rule can provide an exception to the Law of Two to a Scene and to the Law of Contrasts. In this case, two siblings, whether twins or not, can appear at the same time with another character. Romulus and Remus, as well as Castor and Pollux, act as a single individual in the context of oral tradition. Hansel and Gretel, who confront the evil stepmother, the father, and the witch, do so together. Twins (literal or figurative) need not exhibit contrast. Instead they can appear as nearly the same.

7. Importance of Initial and Final Position. Olrik stated that "whenever a series of persons or things occurs, then the principal one will come first. Coming last, though, will be the person for whom the particular narrative arouses sympathy." Thus, it is the younger brother who succeeds where his two older brothers failed. By giving the first position to the oldest brother, the one thought to be the best, the audience is asked to expect success at first. The failure of the two older brothers in contrast with the success of the youngest gives an unexpected result.

8. The Law of the Single Strand. Oral tradition does not use the modern literary device of multiple plot lines interwoven. In contrast, a tale strictly holds to one plot line moving steadily forward. It does not go back in time, and when information from a time before the story is brought in, it is

always done in the dialogue of the characters.

9. Patterning. When there is repetition, the repeated scenes are as similar as possible. When three brothers attempt to confront a monster, they each act in identical ways until the critical moment when the hero – that is the youngest brother – succeeds. When the hero goes to a field three days in a row to fight a giant, each day is identical to the one that proceeds it. This similarity would be unimaginable in modern literature, but it is an important characteristic for oral tradition.

10. The Tableaux Scene. Olrik made the case that during the climactic scene of a tale, in the part he called the Tableaux Scene, the actors of the tale come together for dramatic effect. To illustrate this sort of scene, he described "the hero and his horse; the hero and the monster; Thor pulls the World Serpent up the edge of the boat; the valiant warriors die so near to their king that even in death they protect him." Olrik noted that these are the moments that have so much power, the listener remembers them and the sculptor captures them. He cited the examples of Perseus holding the head of the Medusa or of Sampson among the columns in the hall of the Philistines.

11. The Logic of the Tale. Each theme introduced in a tale must contribute to the plot. In addition, plausibility is measured against the internal logic of the story, not against reality.

12. The Unity of Plot. All the characters and scenes of a tale must contribute to the plot. In addition, there is only one main character.

13. The Ideal Epic Unity. The conflict of the story is apparent from the beginning. Olrik noted that when an unborn child is promised to a monster, the entire story will deal with the consequences of that promise, with rescuing the child from the monster. The various narrative elements may introduce twists, especially when the initial conflict is resolved, but then the story proceeds to a new conflict. In this case, however, the new story is used to further illuminate the relationships of the character. Olrik cited the example of the hero who escapes thanks to the help of the monster's daughter. They flee, but then he forgets her and nearly marries another, only to be reclaimed through her assistance again.

14. Concentration of a Leading Character. When the tale is extremely complex with several stories told in succession, the narrative is held together by its focus on the hero. As Olrik stated: "Only the formal single-strandedness and a certain regard for the character hold the pieces together." When there are two principal characters, there is always a formal protagonist. In the story of the king's son and the monster's daughter, for example, the son is the center of the story and clearly the lead protagonist. The principal character remains the focus throughout the tale. When the choice is between a man and a woman, the man is the protagonist. Ironically, however, the woman often captures the most sympathy, and

while the plot leads with the man, the drama that the woman faces is often of greater interest.

Despite Olrik's turn-of-the-century interpretation of the folktale, stressing its structure rather than its history, the discipline of folklore continued to ask historical questions. For Olrik, a set of rules that described what constrained the folktale did not exclude the possibility that these were traditional forms of oral narrative. In other words, there could be structural rules that governed the form of the folktale, which could still have a history spanning centuries if not millennia. Monographic studies of tale types continued, and hundreds of folklorists contributed to the collective knowledge of the subject.

The challenge to the generally-accepted Finnish Historic Geographic method arose, as discussed above, because questions about the origin of each type did not yield substantial or credible results. In addition, Hitler tainted the idea of a primal Indo-European "Aryan" culture. The significant nail in the coffin came with the long-forgotten work of a Soviet folklorist, published in English in 1958.

As previously described, Vladímir Propp arrived at one of the most important alternative methods to study the folktale. His 1928 *Morphology of the Folktale* has profoundly influenced American folklorists. This is, in part, because of Alan Dundes's important study of American Indian folktales. Dundes (1934-2005) published his dissertation, *The Morphology of North American Indian Folktales* in 1964, and then went on to teach at the University of California, Berkeley. He became an extremely influential folklorist during the last four decades of the twentieth century, particularly because of his ground-breaking study of urban legends. In his study of American Indian folktales, Dundes applied Propp's method with considerable success. It may be, however, that American Indian oral tradition allowed for more flexibility than its European counterpart. Dundes notes that it was possible to record an American folktale from a certain informant, then return years later to the storyteller, only to find many of the motifs in the same tale exchanged for others. This sort of flexibility would have been surprising in a European context.

Propp's approach to the folktale is intriguing, clearly striking credible chords that describe the way the folktale functions. Echoing the work of Olrik, Propp outlines rules by which the folktale operates. It may be a flawed conclusion, however, to see in Propp's ascendancy, the automatic refutation of the idea of traditional folktale types with ancient histories. Olrik's proposal co-existed nicely with historical treatments of the folktale, and Propp's could as well. Perhaps the major obstacle standing in the face of the Finnish method is that pursuing this approach requires a great deal of work. Modern folklore methodology as it is typically practiced in North

America can be done more quickly. A monograph of a folktale type, particularly following the expansion of folklore archives throughout the world, represents a daunting task.

All of this having been said, proponents of the Finnish Historic Geographic method continue to make significant contributions to the field of folklore. More recent attempts to apply genetic theory to the study of the folktale return to biology for insight. Now, considering biology on a molecular level has given a means to use computers to diagram the mutations that occur with a folktale type much as one might study genetic change in a population. Folklorists are hardly prepared to place the idea of the tale type and its history in the dustbin.

A word here about gender analysis of folktales is appropriate. There can be no question that early folklorists viewed oral tradition through a male-dominated lens. James Delargy's famous essay on the Irish storyteller portrayed this professional class as strictly male. In fact, that may have usually been the case when it came to full-time professionals, but the example of Peig Sayers (1873-1958), who provided collectors with such a wealth of stories, makes it clear that Irish women were important purveyors of folklore and could be excellent at the craft of telling stories.

The work of scholars such as Catherine Orenstein, *Little Red Riding Hood Uncloaked: Sex, Morality, and the Evolution of a Fairy Tale* (2008), goes a long way to offering a different way to consider the folktale and oral tradition in general. A word of caution is warranted, however: while some folktales may seem to be within the realm of women because the lead characters are feminine, ethnographic evidence suggests that these were also told by men to mix-gender audiences. Suggesting that women told folktales to girls as a way for addressing things such as puberty is to extrapolate into the past based on ways these stories might have functioned rather than on any clear evidence about the sort of role they actually filled. Since folktales were not generally told to children, there is a problem with suggesting that women told these stories to girls by way of introducing metaphors about maturation.

Gender analysis of oral tradition is a promising frontier for folklore studies. It is nevertheless important to differentiate between projecting models about the way stories "should have" functioned as opposed to concluding the way stories did function based on real evidence. Because of the sexist perspective of early collectors, it may be a challenge to pursue a gender analysis of pre-industrial folklore, but if the line of enquiry is to maintain credibility, it must not stray from the facts.

The Legend

While the folktale was for entertainment, the single episodic legend emphasized the important task of education. The folktale involved the fantastic and the teller did not expect his audience to believe the story. The legend depicts what people believe is true. The telling of a legend may have a role in entertainment, but informing the audience was – and still is – pivotal. Folklorists often use the German term *Sage* (plural *Sagen*) for legend. In Russian, it is *basnya*. In Danish and Norwegian it is *sagn*, a word related to the German word and to the English term "saying." It means basically, "a thing that is told."

Initially, folklorists focused mostly on the folktale because it was assumed to be the oldest form of oral tradition. As discussed, folklorists hoped the genre would reveal a window to peer at an ancient past and to provide the means for the reconstruction of a prehistoric Indo-European religion. Because the legend seemed more recent, it initially received only secondary notice. One of the first scholars to study this part of oral tradition was Henning Frederik Feilberg (1831-1921), representing the generation of European folklorists who followed Jacob Grimm. He was the mentor of Axel Olrik and of the famed Swedish folklorist, Carl Wilhelm von Sydow (1878-1952). Feilberg authored several publications that treated this subject.

It remained, however, for von Sydow to bring the legend to the forefront. Folklorists regard von Sydow as one of the most brilliant theoreticians in the field. After extensive study of the topic, he devised a classification system for the various forms of legends. For his treatment of the subject, see his *Selected Papers of Folklore* (106-126). As the founder of the Ecotype method of folklore studies, von Sydow led the first assault on the standard Finnish Historic Geographic method.

The Ecotype method was in part an answer to the positivists who wanted an approach that would be more verifiable scientifically. Sven S. Liljeblad (1899-2000) was von Sydow's principal student leading the attack in the late 1920s. His study of folktales employing an introduction featuring the Grateful Dead (1927) was an early expression of this method. When Elisabeth Hartmann (1913-2005) arrived from Germany in 1934 to study Swedish folklore, von Sydow and Liljeblad helped shape her research. She was one of the first scholars to apply the Ecotype method to legends. Her study of Scandinavian troll and Celtic fairy beliefs appeared in 1936 and remains a definitive if dated treatment of the subject.

The terms used to classify legends – in large part thanks to von Sydow – include the following categories:

a. The word "dite" was von Sydow's invention as applied to the world of legend. By dite, he meant a short, generally artless recollection without distinct form. It is the core of a legend, but it lacks any of the typical embellishments and trappings of a complete story, serving as it does merely to recall an encounter with the bizarre.

b. Memorates (or memory dites) are brief stories concerning something that the narrator has experienced himself or that was told to him as an actual experience. A story about how the narrator met a deceased loved one or about when she saw a banshee or wood sprite would be a memorate.

c. Etiological legends explain the origin of natural phenomena. The story of God's creating a rainbow as a covenant with humanity after the Great Flood explains the origin of an aspect of nature. Each culture typically has a wide range of etiological legends to explain the origin of fire, land, life, death, and various animals, as well as aspects of culture such as marriage, holiday practices, or even the origin of words. Thus, "OK" allegedly originates with President Andrew Jackson who, according to the story, could not correctly spell the abbreviation of "all correct." Although the use of "OK" predates Jackson, the story survives. People might also explain local items, saying, for example, that a troll angered by Christianity threw a large rock that now rests near a Scandinavian church.

Similarly, the annual migration of lemmings along the steep, ocean-side mountains of Norway resulted in many falling from cliffs and drowning. To explain the seasonal dead that washed ashore, Norwegians recall an etiological legend about lemmings periodically committing collective suicide, racing off cliffs as they followed their leader to their demise, like a "bunch of lemmings," as the phrase maintains. The legend was so powerful and widely accepted that a Disney film crew came to Canada in the late 1950s where they staged an event that appeared as though it were in Norway. The resulting nature documentation went a long way to perpetuate and spread an etiological legend.

d. Testimonial legends are the most-well-developed of these types of stories. More than any other type of *Sagen*, the testimonial legend comes closest in form to *Märchen*. These are lengthy, artistic stories that frequently became traditional, making it possible for folklorists to catalogue and study them in the same way as the folktale. The similarity is so profound that the Grimms included some of these in their *Kinder und Hausmärchen*, and Aarne and Thompson included some in their index of folktale types. The stories of the changeling and of the elves who assist the shoemaker were testimonial legends. In their most elaborate forms, the only thing that differentiates these legends from folktales is that people intend legends to be believed, and even this distinction fails at times as traditional stories shift across the border that only vaguely defines fiction from what some might regard as an account of an actual occurrence. Shared motifs, structure, and general narrative style can further blur the distinction, but the intended veracity of the story is the critical means to segregate the testimonial legend from the folktale.

The Norwegian scholar Reidar Th. Christiansen, building on the work of von Sydow, published his important book, *The Migratory Legends*, in 1958, identifying dozens of testimonial legend types. Many of these stories are well known because they are so widely diffused. Elves steal a baby, leaving a changeling in its place. The suspicious mother tricks the creature into revealing its identity as an old elf, and her real baby is returned. A man riding home late at night meets a woman who offers him a drink from a golden goblet. Suspicious, he takes the cup but throws the liquid behind him, searing the hair from the horse's rump. He then charges into the dark, pursued by an angry mob of fairies. By crossing a bridge, he barely makes his escape, cup in hand to prove that his exploit really occurred. These stories were intended to demonstrate why it was important to believe in a wide range of supernatural beings, providing guidance about how to behave when they were encountered.

e. Historical legends can be as elaborate and artistic as testimonial legends. In fact, they often are testimonial legends that have been attached to historical personages, events, or places. Regardless of their specific form, these legends are associated with historically-known people or events. Although they sometimes partially rest on accurate depictions of the past, they are generally pure fiction attached to prominent people of historic significance. William Tell, Joan of Arc, King Richard the Lionheart, Napoleon, George Washington, Dolly Madison, Abraham Lincoln, the Beatles, and practically every other prominent person in history has attracted legendary material.

The various supernatural beings associated with legends are discussed in the following chapter. At this point, however, it is appropriate to proceed with an overview of the remaining forms of oral narrative.

The Medieval Ballad

Today, people use the word "ballad" to signify a wide variety of songs, but originally, the genre emerged in western European during the so-called twelfth-century renaissance, a time of dynamic creativity. Members of the nobility promulgated the ballad as an art form. Later, the peasantry adopted it. Throughout most of its history, the ballad was intended as dance music, the term itself deriving from the Latin word *ballare* meaning "to dance," from which we have the term "ballet." Folklorists recognize the following forms of ballad:

a. Historical ballads. These were perhaps the original form of western European ballad, and they are in nature like historical legends.

b. <u>Mythological ballads</u>. These are, in content, the counterpart of testimonial legends.

c. <u>Religious ballads</u>. The subject matter of these songs deals principally with martyred saints. These, too, have a counterpart in legends.

d. <u>Humorous ballads</u>. This is youngest form of ballad. These have a counterpart Aarne's classification of fictional tales, "Jokes and Anecdotes," Type numbers 1200-1999.

While the ballad is a genre of folklore, it is yet another means to express the same ideas that are most at home in the legend. Nineteenth-century folklorists contributed a great deal of effort collecting and organizing ballads before modernization extinguished them in oral tradition. One of the more famous published collections of ballads is F. J. Child's *English and British Popular Ballads*, published in five volumes between 1882 and 1898. Axel Olrik was drawn to the subject, following a trend that directed folklorists to find ways to deal with aspects of oral tradition other than the folktale.

The One-Strophic Folk Lyric

In contrast with the ballad, the one-strophic folk lyric was traditional with the peasantry, rather than invented by the aristocracy. This form of song was brief, usually consisting of four versus. They were typically dance songs and they were common throughout the Old World.

Other Forms of Oral Narrative

Riddles and jokes are additional forms of oral narrative. The riddle is ancient in the Old World, following a well-established formula consisting of an ambiguous description. "Box without lid; gold within" is one of the oldest European riddles, and it appears in literature. The answer is an egg. For some cultures, the idea of the riddle is an absurdity, while for others it is a time-honored game.

The joke is a widespread genre with old roots. European peasantry told numskull stories and other humorous tales for centuries. Other traditional jokes make fun of wives or parsons. These stories appear in Aarne and Thompson's Tale Type Index. Type 1365A, for example, describes a husband and wife who are arguing. The woman falls into a river and drowns. The husband looks for her body upstream, since he assumes that she will have drifted against the current because of her contrary disposition. Gender jokes appear to be some of the oldest representatives in this genre.

Because of its diversity, the United States provided fertile soil for the growth of a wide variety of jokes about dialects and ethnicity. Europeans developed some jokes along these lines, making fun of Jews, for example. In addition, jokes about neighboring ethnic groups are not uncommon, but North America with its ever-plentiful supply of immigrants seemed to always have the available material for a new cycle of jokes, or to apply old jokes to new victims.

A politically-correct, "PC" society, however, has extinguished many forms of jokes. Minority and gender jokes have dropped into a subculture of humor or have disappeared altogether. Those groups of people not protected by PC politics allow for acceptable outlets, and many of the traditional jokes once cruelly applied to some groups have been adapted to permissible targets. The stupid white male remains an allowable brunt of the joke. Such jokes are also used against regions or states without triggering a PC rebuff.

Jokes remain to be adequately handled by folklorists. It is an enormous field, particularly in view of the on-going creativity of the folk in the twentieth-first century. When folktales and many legend types are no longer told, there will still be jokes.

Chapter 9 Supernatural beings

Traditional beliefs and customs identified means to placate supernatural beings. In addition, folktales employ them as devices in stories, but it is the legend that gives these creatures definition, providing explanation and detail about what is believed. Liljeblad provides four general questions that can be asked about supernatural beings in popular belief:

   1. <u>What type of supernatural being is discussed in legends?</u> The folk believed in what Liljeblad called "death beings" such as ghosts, souls, or the walking dead as opposed to nature beings, often called "the owners of nature." Some legends exhibit only a vague border between these two groups, and the same story, told in different places, may employ one or the other. Determining the type of supernatural being that a legend describes is an important first step.
   2. <u>How are the owners of nature depicted?</u> The folk have always seen the world as inhabited by a wide variety of nature beings. Some are singular and isolated and others are social. It is important to exercise caution here since singular, isolated beings occasionally appear in pairs or triplets, but they still function as single entities. Three beautiful water sprites acting in concert function as an isolated character in belief and story. True social supernatural owners of nature are rare internationally. People perceive them as appearing in family groups, living in communities that mirror the human condition. This sort of belief is largely restricted to Northern Europe, Polynesia, and Russia to a certain extent.
   3. <u>What part of the world does the supernatural being own?</u> It is important to identify where these creatures live and what they command. The rulers or owners of nature, in the purest sense of the idea, are usually isolated. Social beings are more typically free-roving and less attached to a specific location. Traditional isolated entities command specific locations

such as the forest, a lake or stream, the sea, or a mountain. The concept is often applied as well to a house, a mill, or other man-made sites, but these domestic beings behave in the same way as an owner of nature. Modern counterparts include the World War II gremlins who inhabited airfields and airplanes. Similarly, the modern extraterrestrial owns outer space. Western American tradition adopted the Cornish knocker, the owner of the mine, and there are many other examples.

4. How does the supernatural being function in legend? Originally, many of these creatures were probably thought to be actual creators of various aspects of nature, but with Christianization, God jealously guarded the act of creation. Still, Northern Europeans often believed that giants, who are in fact merely large supernatural social beings, created various features in the natural world. The folk sometimes also thought that other supernatural beings created specific aspects of the world. In addition, there is the question about how the supernatural beings interacted with humanity. They could be regarded as helpful or dangerous. In non-European cultures, they can also assume the role of promoters of evil. Most legends focus on the horrific and terrifying since morbid and dangerous topics are typically more intriguing than the opposite.

The preceding questions are important when organizing legendary depictions of the supernatural since there are often contradictions and overlaps. Any summary of types of supernatural beings places them into groups that may not have been universally agreed upon by the folk, with all its diversity across time and space. The amorphous quality of oral tradition creates contradictions, ambiguities, and change. The following generalizations, however, offered guidelines.

Death and Soul Beliefs

1. Ghosts. People tells stories about the dead appearing before the living perhaps in all cultures, but there are several forms they can assume. Some cultures emphasize animated corpses and that the dead can bodily rise from the grave and walk the earth. Others have traditions involving the dead appearing only as disembodied spirits. Most people think of the dead in human form. This is a requirement for animated corpses, but it is also a general assumption about spirits. There are, nevertheless, legends of souls and ghosts appearing as animals.

The attitude of the dead can be hostile or favorable to the living. The farther east one goes in Europe, the more likely that the dead will be hostile to the living. In general, walking corpses do little good, but the spirits of the dead, while sometimes benevolent, can also be dangerous. Legends about the dead should be considered along these lines. In modern North America, ghosts are generally spirits in human form, and in folk tradition they usually are good-willed toward the living. Films and literature contradict this by often depicting the dead as perilous for the sake of drama.

The Lenore Legend is one of the older and more widespread stories about the dead. It was so well known that Aarne and Thompson include it in their folktale index (Type 365), even though it is more often told as a legend, that is, to be believed. In the story, a young bride waits for the return of her betrothed who has gone off to war. Other soldiers come home, but not the man she loves. One night, he appears before her and asks her to leave with him. Delighted to see him, she climbs up behind him on his horse, and they ride quickly across the moonlit landscape. At one point, his horse jumps over a creek or some other obstacle, and he pitches forward, revealing that the skin has been sheared off the back of his head, and his white skull shines bright in the moonlight. In other variants, his bride looks down at a stream they are crossing, and in the moonlight, she sees their reflection, revealing her companion to be a rotting corpse. Just as they reach his open grave, she jumps from the horse, saving herself. Her bridegroom returns to his grave, which supernaturally closes. The woman lives to tell her tale, but in many variants, she dies soon after from the shock.

Gottfried August Bürger (1747-1794) made this story famous with his 1773 poem, "Lenore." Within a decade after its publication, the German-language masterwork appeared in English translation, becoming an immediate sensation: it is credited with influencing Coleridge, Wordsworth, and other British poets of the newly-emerging Romantic era. In addition, the fame of Bürger's poem and the association of the name "Lenore" with all things morbid may have influenced Edgar Allen Poe to write his own poem, "Lenore," and to feature the name in some of his other works.

The story appears to have considerable age as evidenced by the Old Norse story from *The Poetic Edda*, the "Second Lay of Helgi the Hunding-Slayer/Helgakviða Hundingsbana II." This describes how Helgi, a dead hero, returns from the grave on a horse to beckon his beloved, Sigrún, for one last night of conjugal bliss. The document suggests that originally the story may have played out differently: Sigrún willingly enters Helgi's burial mound to lie with him. The poem subsequently relates that the heroine "lived but a short while longer, for grief and sorrow." With this, the medieval text returns to the conclusion found in its more recent counterpart. This example suggests that for pre-Christian society, crossing the line into the supernatural – or at least in this case into the realm of the dead – for romance was heroic. Nineteenth-century expressions of the story generally assert that no living person would want to enter the grave, even when it is the last resting place of a lover. In a Christian context, the living must have no greater love than the one reserved for God, and to choose death runs against Christian teaching.

2. Souls. The belief that the soul can travel outside the body in one form or another, before or after death, is widespread. Legends describe the ability of someone spiritually communicating with another person over great distances, which modern North Americans give a scientific veneer, using the term "telepathy." There are other legends that depict the soul of the living in corporeal form. In addition, there is a question as to whether a person has one or more souls. The ancient Egyptians firmly believed that people possessed two souls, and much of the mummification ceremony consisted of the magical protection of these two entities with their distinct needs.

Old Norse sagas describe the concept of the *fylgja*, which means "the follower." This was a double spirit that acted as a guardian, appearing in dreams with warnings. The belief is not unlike the modern concept of the guardian angel, but traditions and beliefs vary as to whether this spirit is part of the person or was granted to the person as a divine gift, presumably at birth.

There are many examples of the soul appearing as an animal. In the Old Norse saga of Hrolf Kraka, King Hrolf fights his last, greatest battle, but Bothvar Bjarki, his best warrior, is asleep and cannot be awoken. A large, ferocious bear, however, fights for the king. Finally, Bjarki awakens and enters the battle, but the bear disappears.

Souls can also appear as shadows. Legends tell of people who have done extraordinarily evil deeds and no longer cast shadows. Their souls have already gone to hell.

Legends about souls appearing during life, at the time of death, and after death are some of the most tenacious in the modern world. Where people once believed that the soul of living people could appear in animal form, the modern world typically conceives of it as invisible but capable of traveling without the body. One of the most widespread modern legends deals with the supernatural communication of death or injury by the traveling soul. My own family has two of these stories, both involving World War II. My father was in England before the invasion of Normandy in 1944, and he met an English family who had lost their son in combat. They explained that they had known the moment of his death because his picture on the mantel suddenly fell over with no explanation. His mother said she immediately understood this to mean that her son had died.

While my father-in-law was fighting in Europe, he was wounded in the hand. Family oral tradition maintains that at that very moment (the exact moment, of course, would be difficult to verify), his mother, sitting at the dinner table in Iowa, felt a pain in her hand. She immediately announced, "Donald has been hurt."

Legends like these are repeated thousands of times in the modern world. They reveal the on-going belief in the ability of the soul to transcend space and death.

Supernatural Beings of Nature

1. <u>Isolated Beings.</u> A wide variety of supernatural beings are regarded as rulers of specific aspects of nature. Before conversion, people may have regarded them as creating those features, although the protector of a forest, pond, or any other thing does not necessarily have that role. In Scandinavia, the spirit guarding the forest is often thought to be a female, while the one in custody of water is male. Exceptions abound. In Sweden, these rulers of nature are known as *rå*, so that a *skogsrå* rules the forest, the *sjorå* rules the lake, and so on.

In Classical mythology, Artemis/Diana played the role of the guardian of the forest, presiding over the hunt. By implication, she could choose the animals a hunter could kill and which were to remain alive. The image of this goddess is consistent with the commonly held Northern European perspective that the wood sprite is a young, beautiful, and even seductive woman. The modern image of Mother Nature is consistent with this portrait, appearing as a supernatural being who is often more enticing than maternal.

Occasionally, the wood sprite has a hideous feature. In Scandinavia, she may have the tail of a cow or a hollow back. There are many legends of a lonely hunter or a charcoal burner who is easily seduced by this sprite, only to recognize the danger by eventually noticing the remarkable, unnatural feature. Such stories often employ an ancient motif. When the wood sprite asks for the hunter's name, he is suspicious of her and replies "No Man" or "Self." He then thrusts a burning piece of wood into the hollow of her back and runs away.

The wood sprite screams, and a voice calls out from deep within the forest asking what is wrong. She then answers, "Self burnt me." The voice in the forest then replies, "If you burnt yourself, you have yourself to blame." Folklorists refer to this as the "Polyphemus legend" after the famous, similar incident in the *Odyssey*.

As mentioned above, spirits ruling lakes and rivers are usually male in Scandinavia. These spirits appear in animal or human form, but often they change between the two at will. In Northern Europe, they frequently manifested as an old fiddler of great skill. People suspected talented human musicians of having learned from this supernatural mentor at some great price. When transposed into a Christian context, the folk often regarded the spirit as the devil, who had purchased the soul of the musician in exchange for his incredible ability. The Northern European water sprite also appears as a horse, and there are many legends involving human interaction with this strong, unnatural – and dangerous – beast.

Lakes can also be regarded as an ill-defined spirit without animal or human form. A widespread European legend tells of a person who is standing by a lake on New Year's Eve and hears a voice call out, "the hour has come, but not the man." At that point, a man riding a charging horse plunges into the lake and drowns. The idea behind this legend is that the lake requires a human death once a year. In a year when there had not been a drowning, the lake demanded a price. At the last minute, the lake spirit used its supernatural ability to call on a horse to deliver its rider to pay the annual debt. Christiansen catalogued this as Migratory Legend 4050, "The hour is come but the man is not."

Figure 8. Thirteenth-century mermaid. Misericords are small benches on the underside of choir seats, which when turned up for standing, still offered support during long services. Fantastic beasts from folklore often serve as brackets for the benches. This example is from Wells Cathedral in Britain. The hand holding the comb has broken, the mirror remains.

Spirits of the sea take several forms, but the stereotypical image is that of the mermaid (literally, "sea woman"), who is half human, half fish. Like the forest sprite, she often had erotic qualities, playing into the female-starved life of the sailor. The mermaid caused storms and other problems for sailors, and she frequently enticed men to their watery deaths in her embrace. It is possible, however, to win her favor, at which point she can be helpful.

The mermaid is normally shown combing her hair and holding or looking into a mirror. After conversion to Christianity, clerics interpreted this motif as an expression of the beautiful spirit's vanity, a sign of her eternal damnation. The mirror and comb may link her to a variety of supernatural beings who have custody of the dead. There is an ancient European tradition of the older women in society washing the dead and combing the hair of corpses. The comb can consequently be understood as having been associated with death. The mirror, with its eerie, unnatural ability to reflect the world, was also an obvious metaphor for death as a reflection of life. The Irish banshee combs her hair as she howls, heralding death in an old Irish family. Ancient Pictish stones from Scotland may use a comb and mirror as symbols to refer to the deceased.

The mermaid's practice of combing her hair and looking in a mirror may refer to one of her lost functions in relation to the dead. Many Northern European traditions depict the dead as traveling across the sea. The Scandinavian myth of the return of the dead aboard *Naglfar*, the ship made of dead-men's nails, is part of this tradition. There are also many legends that survived conversion to Christianity, which refer to concerns for those lost at sea. These special dead, untended by the living with funerals and burials, survive in the supernatural world ruled by the mermaid. As with so much of the more deeply rooted traditions, it is only possible to speculate about the links that may or may not exist. Motifs may have meant something specific before conversion to Christianity, but lacking clear primary sources, speculation dominates the process of interpretation. And it is important to remember that a motif that meant one thing two millennia ago, could have meant another five hundred years ago, and it could refer to something completely different one hundred and fifty years ago. And when it is reinterpreted in a Disney film in the late twentieth century, the motif can transform again. Folklorists can document the current belief system, and are too often left to speculate about the past.

In addition to the mermaid, there are legends that depict mermen, but these are less widespread, and they invariably are linked to the Northern European belief in social beings. Mermen are usually part of social organizations that reflect human communities. This concept manifests clearly in those areas where belief in seal people replaces that of half-human, half-fish merfolk. Scotland and the islands to the north and west, and parts of Northern Ireland manifest legends about people who shed seal skins to appear as humans, only to return to their animal skins to live in the ocean.

Figure 9. The Pictish memorial stone from Dunnichen (Angus), modern-day Scotland, likely dates to the second half of the first millennium, CE. W. A. Cummins sees the text as including two symbols plus a mirror and comb. He translates it as a stylized plant symbol for an unidentified name – meaning "son of" – above a double disc and Z-rod, which he identifies as the name Drust or Drosten. Cummins further translates the comb and mirror as meaning "Rest in Peace" or "here lies."

People throughout Europe believed that a guardian spirit, yet another isolated supernatural being, occupied their houses. In England, these are brownies; in Denmark, *nisse*; in Sweden, *tomte*; and in Russia, *domovoi*. The creature is almost always male, appearing as a little old man, often in shabby clothes and a red cap. He is usually benevolent, working for the success of the household and foretelling disaster. In return, the spirit demanded respect and a token amount of food and cast-off clothes on holidays. There are numerous legends regarding these creatures. Many involve the house spirit punishing an ungrateful peasant.

A well-known story, classified as Migratory Legend 7015, "The New Suit," involves a husband and wife who knew that many chores were being done during the night. They wanted to see who was responsible for this kindness, so they hid themselves in the barn and watched. They were impressed to see a *nisse*, but they noticed that he wore tattered clothes that barely sheltered him from the cold. Feeling sorry for him and being grateful for what the little fellow had done for them, the man and woman left the creature a fine set of white pants and a new shirt. For several days after leaving him the gift, the people saw that the *nisse* had not completed any of the chores. Finally, the man stayed in the barn to see if he could catch another glimpse of the creature. He found him leaning against a post, his hands thrust into the pockets of his new pair of pants. "Why have you not done your chores?" asked the man. "You don't expect me to ruin my fine new clothes, do you?" answered the *nisse*. And that was the last the people saw of the spirit or of his good deeds.

This legend, which appears in everything from the collection of the Brothers Grimm to the Harry Potter series, serves as a warning not to spy on the house spirit and not to express gratitude in ways that are excessive or not tied to the holidays.

2. Social Beings. As explained above, supernatural beings living in human-like communities are relatively rare. They occur in the traditions of Polynesia, Britain and Ireland, Scandinavia, Iceland and the North Sea islands, and to a certain extent the Russia. The Celts may have influenced Scandinavian traditions since the two groups had millennia-old contact. In English, the supernatural beings were traditionally called "elves," but in the Celtic areas they are more typically referred to as "fairies." In Gaelic, they are the *sidhe* (pronounced "shee"). The Norwegians call them *huldre* meaning hidden. In Sweden they are the trolls, but the country is enormous and various locations used different terms. The geographic distribution and history of the word "troll" is extremely complex since it can refer to a wide variety of supernatural beings, depending on the location, and it is sometimes used generically for many types of supernatural beings.

There are abundant legends about human contact with these supernatural beings, and the outcome is usually negative. The entities seek to steal food and to abduct people. Women and small children – particularly boys – are most vulnerable. Some stories also recount a man who happens into a fairy ring, a dancing circle of elves, and falls into their spell.

The story of fairies who steal a human infant and leave an ugly changeling was so popular that its distribution exceeds even the belief in social supernatural beings. A solitary supernatural woman or a witch takes the place of the community of fairies in those areas where such a tradition did not exist. An example of witches abducting an infant in the same way as fairies occurs in the *Satyricon* by the first-century Roman writer Titus Petronius Arbiter. And Martin Luther famously described another changeling.

There are numerous popular legends dealing with various aspects of the social supernatural beings. Migratory Legend 5070, "The Midwife and the Fairies," describes how one night a man came to the door of a human midwife and asked for help. She did not recognize him, even though she thought she knew everyone in the area, but she put on her shawl and followed him into the dark. Unsure of where she was going, either because of fog or some other device, she and the man finally arrived at a little cottage. Inside, a woman was attempting to give birth, but there were complications. The midwife saved the mother and infant. The man gave the midwife a salve for the baby's eyes, with the warning not to get any of it into her own eyes. She tried to obey but accidentally rubbed one of her eyes before cleaning her hands. The man and the new mother thanked the midwife for her services and paid her richly, and then the man returned her to her house.

The next day, the midwife was at the market, and she happened to see the man from the night before taking food from the various stands without paying. She followed him, and then finally addressed him, asking why he was stealing from the merchants. At first, he was surprised until he recognized her from the night before. "With which eye do you see me?" he asked. The midwife indicated one eye or the other, at which point the man, who was in fact a fairy, wiped her eye with his finger, taking with him her supernatural vision. In darker versions, the man blinds the midwife in her affected eye.

In recognition of the dangers involved, people exercised extreme caution when dealing with or referring to these supernatural beings. Because of their ability to be invisible, fairies could be anywhere and were likely to be listening to any conversation that involved them, inspiring people to speak about them with proper deference. It was extremely important to use *noa* names rather than taboo names, which would anger the "good neighbors." The social supernatural beings assumed radically different forms depending on the culture.

Personification

Some concepts, such as death and fortune, are given human attributes and appear in folktales and legends. The extraordinary circumstance of the fourteenth-century Black Death inspired stories that could be collected five centuries later. These incorporated a personification of the disease in the form of a brother and sister known as pest boy and pest girl. It is possible that these characters predate the Black Death, but the monumental nature of that plague served as a powerful magnet that attached itself to the motif.

The use of personifications of abstract ideas is more common in Eastern Europe where day and night, the seven days of the week, or the twelve months of the year frequently appear in folktales. The Romans took this practice to an extreme, creating allegorical personifications of a wide variety of concepts. In the Classical world, Justice and various arts became minor deities – or muses – that still survive. Most of these were not a matter of widespread belief, but they nevertheless figure in stories of various sorts.

The United States of America employs several of these including Liberty, America, Columbia, and Uncle Sam. Such characters do not appear in legend since they are symbolic and are not believed to be real, but they are nevertheless powerful images.

Supernatural beings that are like soul beliefs

The nightmare and the werewolf are two creatures that deal with the human spirit in a way different from other beliefs related to the soul. People believed that these were the products of bizarre transformations endured by innocent people who are unaware of the circumstance. While the nightmare was a traveling spirit of a woman, the curse of the werewolf affected men. In both cases, European peasants regarded them as victims of witchcraft. The cause of their suffering was that their mothers had used magical means to avoid the pains of childbirth, leaving their children to suffer these unnatural afflictions.

In the case of the nightmare, while a woman "went mare," as it was called, she traveled the land to plague others. She frequently appeared as a mouse that would sit upon the chests of men, giving them horrible dreams.

There are many legends dealing with this motif. One tells of a young man who repeatedly suffers from a nightmare. His mother searched the house and found an opening large enough for a mouse. That night, when her son was in the throes of a nightmare, she plugged the hole and put a pot over the boy's chest. The next morning, she removed the pot. A mouse jumped off the boy and transformed into a beautiful young woman. That very day, a woman in a nearby village died before waking.

Some variants of this elaborate story – Migratory Legend 4010, "Married to the Nightmare" – go on to tell how the young man married this strange visitor. They lived a happy life until one day the woman and her mother-in-law quarreled and the old woman told her daughter-in-law how she arrived in the household. She then removed the plug from the wall, and the young woman changed into a mouse and disappeared forever.

This echoes a motif usually found in folktales – which are sometimes told as legends – involving the magical bride captured because her garment of swan wings or seal skin is taken and hidden by the hero. One day, the woman finds her hidden magical wings or skin, and she is compelled to return to her former shape and life. This was an ancient story that combined with the idea of the nightmare.

The werewolf was the male counterpart of the nightmare. While this cursed man sleeps, his spirit travels the land in the shape of a wolf. Unlike the nightmare, who merely gave bad dreams, the werewolf kills livestock and people, having a special affinity for pregnant women. Like the nightmare, the man sleeps unaware that his soul prowls the land in animal form. His identity is discovered when he is wounded in wolf form or someone calls out his name. Werewolf stories can conclude with the disenchantment of the man, but some also end with his death.

The idea of the werewolf draws on a much older belief in shape shifting. There is clear evidence of a widespread European tradition that people, and especially men, intentionally took animal forms through magical means or special talent. This belief appears in the *Satyricon*, the first-century Roman work of Petronius, described above. In this story, a soldier who is a *versipellis*, a skin-changer or werewolf, is walking among some tombstones one night when he removes his clothes and urinates around them. The clothes turn to stone, and the soldier becomes a wolf. That night a wolf kills some sheep, but a slave tending the animals pierces the wolf in the neck. The next day, the soldier, in human form, is found to have a wound in his neck.

Christiansen classifies stories of this kind as Migratory Legend 4005, "the Werewolf Husband," in which a man's wife discovers that her husband is a werewolf as indicated by wounds that he has received. The act of recognition releases the man from the spell. Ella Odstedt in her *Varulven i Svensk Folktradition* (1943) describes three principal ways in which a man becomes a wolf: the man's mother had magically avoided pain in childbirth, and this brought a curse on her child; a curse is magically placed on a man by another person; or the werewolf actively and magically brings about his own transformation. Odstedt suggests that the last of these causes is the oldest. Dag Strömbäck supports this suggestion. He further points out in his *Folklore och Filologi* (1970) that Old Norse sources confirm the idea that men magically caused their own change.

Icelandic sagas give considerable details about men who caused their own transformations into wolves and bears; *ulfheðin* and *berserkr*, respectively. These terms, which literally mean "wolf coats" and "bear shirts," refer to the belief that men could either cause their actual transformation or that they could magically acquire the attributes of the ferocious animals by wearing their skin and going into a trance. Such men were feared in battle because they believed that neither fire nor steel could harm them. According to tradition, these men thought themselves to be invincible, and so they charged into battle recklessly. Most of Scandinavia outlawed the practice of going "berserk" because people regarded the act to be dangerous, destructive, and generally anti-social. The sagas describe heroes who confront groups of berserkers and defeat them with great difficulty. Whether these literary accounts and records of laws indicate that some men actually believed they could transform themselves is a matter of dispute. Accounts of witches and laws against witchcraft do not mean that there were witches. On the other hand, there were certainly people who felt they could use magic for a variety of purposes. By analogy, there may have been men who felt they had the power to transform into bears or wolves.

Figure 10. A thirteenth-century ivory chess piece from the Isle of Lewis off the coast of Scotland depicts a Viking *berserkr*, as indicated by the biting of the shield. These feared warriors believed they turned into bears in battle and were invincible to fire or steel. Kings placed them on the flanks of armies, and so in chess, this piece represents a rook. This example is from the Scottish National Museum.

There is evidence that Marie de France, a twelfth-century author from the nobility, helped spread the idea of the cursed werewolf who cannot control his own magical change. She wrote a widely-distributed story containing this motif. Because of the power of the written word in folk tradition, Marie de France may have had a role in changing the story as popularly told, making the werewolf the victim of magic as her version ascended in importance over the older tradition of a man intentionally changing himself.

Other entities that recall traditions associated with the soul include the familiars or spirit servants of witches. Familiars can appear in any number of forms including cats, rabbits, and pigs. There is some ambiguity as to whether these creatures are demons associated with the witch or that they are the witch herself or a familiar created by the witch.

There are legends that describe witches making what is called a carrying doll. This was a bundle of stolen items mixed with blood from the witch's left hand. The object then became a familiar with the capacity to turn into a variety of animate shapes. It was generally believed that the owner of such a fetish was doomed to eternal damnation. The only escape was to sell it for less than it was purchased, and with each sale, it grew in strength. Thus, the carrying doll with the greatest power was purchased with a grain of sand.

Isolated beings that are like the owners of nature

While the female sprite dominates the forest, there is also an important group of beliefs involving male rulers of the forest. Medieval literature has many references to wild men, fur-covered custodians of animals and trees. It was a widespread belief throughout Europe that the forest was inhabited either by these wild men or by creatures that were half goat and half man. The latter were good-natured but mischievous with an exaggerated sexual appetite. The ancient Greeks called the creature Pan, which became the root for one of the personifications of the devil after conversion. This is why the devil is frequently depicted with goat legs, and indeed, Pan was a *noa* name, a safe way to refer to the devil in medieval times.

Numerous historians have referred to this bas-relief as a male Celtic Medusa, comparing it to the Greek gorgon whose stare could turn people to stone. The Medusa plays an important role in the story of Perseus and Andromeda, and she is well known as having hair full of snakes. The association of the image from Bath with the Medusa is not clearly justified. Two snakes are visible in the lower third of the carving, and there may be more surrounding the face. Even the two feathered wings behind each ear are frequently found with Medusa, seeming to confirm the interpretation.

Romans frequently combined Classical and regional deities, and this may be what this represents. The face from Aquae Sulis also has the appearance of the ruler of the forest, the master of the animals. The idea that different areas had a dominant entity who held sway over creatures of the woods is ancient. It is echoed in the medieval tradition of the wild man and the green man with manes of disheveled hair, living in the forest and acted as its guardian. The antiquity of the motif finds expression in Enkidu, the wild man and companion of Gilgamesh, the hero of ancient Mesopotamia.

Figure 11. Roman-era stone face at the ritual springs at Aquae Sulis (the Waters of Sulis), Bath, England, is of uncertain meaning. The hot spring was sacred even before the Romans built a large complex at the site. Sulis was an important Celtic deity associated with water and healing. The Celts have had a long history of regarding springs as sacred, and there is considerable archaeological evidence of people throwing coins and other sacrificed objects into Aquae Sulis. The tradition of the sacred spring is preserved in the form of today's wishing well.

This entity transformed into an all-purpose, elf-like trickster, equally at home in the human world as in the forest. The Irish referred to the Pan character as *pucca*, an ancestor of Puck who figures in literature, including Shakespeare's plays. Related characters give evidence of the wide distribution of this name. For the Welsh, it was *bucca*, for the Latvians the house sprite was *pukis*, and for the Swedes, the familiar of a witch was *puke*.

Internationally, there are many variations of creatures linked with nature, some of whom behave in ways that are reminiscent of the owners of nature without fitting the strictest definition. In North America's Great Basin, Northern Paiute tradition includes the *paúngaa'a*, which translates as "water baby," a name that does not match the sinister quality of the creature. This ruler of the water plays an important role in a testimonial legend that tells of a woman who left her infant in a cradleboard by the water while she gathered edible plants. She hears her infant crying, and so she returns and attempts to suckle the baby. When the baby opens its mouth, it reveals huge fangs, and it bites into the breast of the woman. It is, in fact, the *paúngaa'a*, which has devoured the baby and is now chewing on the mother. The woman must quickly summon a shaman with *paúngaa'a* power to chant the demon away. The supernatural being responds by retreating back into the water. This legend warns about the dangers of the water and about not being an attentive mother. To achieve this, it calls on the belief in a ruler of the water.

Social beings that are like elves

The belief in giants is widespread throughout the world. These beings are generally at home in etiological legends, playing roles in the creation of the world or its specific features. They also serve as adversaries of gods or heroes. The Greek word for giant was *gigantos*, meaning huge. Scandinavian languages use variations of *gjette*, which literally means "big eater." Most of the Celtic lands do not have a true giant, the Cornish being a notable exception. When adapting a foreign story with such a character, the Celts typically employed a large ogre called a *gruagach*.

Europeans regard giants as belonging to a former time, having long since died out or moved away. Legends recount the giants' past exploits, frequently referring to features in the landscape as evidence of their former existence.

There is a widespread European belief in supernatural women who determine the fate of humanity. Each had a name that referred to past, present, and future, and not surprisingly, it was the entity that governed the future that inspired the most interest. In English, they were called the weird sisters, using the word *wyrd*, the Old English future tense of the verb "to be." The name for the entity in charge of the future was applied to all three collectively.

The Romans referred to these goddesses as *Fata* (plural *Fatae*) as derived from *fatum*, the word for fate. This root is often linked with the term *fey*, a word imported into English that presumably serves as the basis for "fairy," although the exact etymology of the term is disputed.

For the ancient Greeks, the three fates were called *Moirae*, and in Old Norse they were *Norns*. Besides being the wardens of past, present, and future, they were also the goddesses of birth, life, and death. These entities did not persist in any clear way in the folklore of the nineteenth century, but there are indications of the tradition in pagan times and vestiges of the folklore survive to the present. These motifs, references that have lost their contextual meaning, are known as "blind motif."

The fates were the weavers of destiny. Icelandic sagas describe them literally as working looms, determining who will die and who will live, making a range of detailed choices as they wove their eerie cloth. Their loom was made of dead men's bones. The fabric was of intestines, and skulls served as the weights to keep the weave tight and orderly. This may be more of a literary device than reflecting actual belief, but there is no doubt that these creatures inspired fear and awe. It is no mistake that the three weird sisters of Shakespeare's "Scottish Play" (in theatrical circles, it is regarded as bad luck to give voice to the name of the play "Macbeth") spoke of the future. The fates toyed with humanity, laughing as foolish mortals struggled against the women's inevitable design of the future.

It is also worth noting that, in general, pre-industrial Europeans regarded the future as consisting of more of the same, except that some bad things were likely to happen. The idea of a steady decay of humanity and existence is present in the Bible where one finds the "fall of man," with the exile from Eden, after which, people inherited less and less of the lost immortality and nobility of Adam, causing lives to become progressively shorter and more miserable. Since with every generation, people were one step more removed from Adam (and by implication, from God), all sorts of good qualities were in decline. The past was generally perceived as better than the present, and by implication, if the future were to vary at all from the present, it would be worse. The remnants of massive building projects of ancient civilizations were attributed either to giants from long past or to the superhuman efforts of extraordinary people "back then," the likes of which did not exist in the present and were not likely to be seen in a declining future.

Also regarding the perception of the future in Europe after conversion, there was a general assumption that the Second Coming of Jesus was imminent. So, unless one was among the select few taken by the "Rapture," the prospects of the near future were fairly grim, as outlined by the New Testament Book of Revelation. The belief is preserved to this day among some groups who are ever-ready to predict the immediate return of Jesus.

Legendary characters that are like condemned souls

Europeans were fascinated by the idea of condemned souls, either of individuals or groups of people, who could not find rest. These unfortunates were forced to exist in a nether world, appearing occasionally before the living as evidence of their hideous or peculiar plight. Such motifs have been favorites with artists and writers. It is possible to identify six types of these beings.

1. The "Wild Hunt" is probably the oldest, occurring in ancient Greek sources and Scandinavian mythology. A cluster of stories refers to ghostly riders who race across the landscape or the night sky, questing for some phantom quarry that they can never catch. Legends tell of people seeing this eerie phenomenon. There are occasional references to the leader as being the god of death.

2. The "Sleeping Army" is a motif that appears in a variety of stories telling of a group of warriors killed in combat, who haunt the battlefield or wait inside a mound for some future conflict. People often believe such an army serves as a matter of last resort, a supernatural force that will awaken if their country is threatened with destruction. King Arthur's knights are often regarded as sleeping in this way, waiting for the return of their king, healed from his wounds after recuperating in the western island of Avalon.

3. The "Flying Dutchman" is one of the better known and often used motifs of the condemned souls. This motif describes a phantom ship of ghostly sailors who travel the seas but never find harbor or rest. Their only respite comes once every century, when they are allowed to anchor at a legendary port. Their ship is seen in bad weather. The story seems to be of medieval origin.

4. The "Wandering Jew" is also a motif belonging to this class. Like the Flying Dutchman, the Wandering Jew appears to be of medieval origin. The legend tells of Ahasverus, a shoemaker of Jerusalem who refused to allow Jesus to sit while carrying his cross to Calvary. His fate is to wander the world, longing for rest.

5. The Will-'o-the-Wisp is described in Chapter 4. The character was not good enough for heaven and made himself feared by the devil, and so he was exiled from hell. He carries a burning ember, a relic from the time when he briefly entered the abode of Satan, and with this phantom light, he lures nighttime travelers away from their destination. This character is common in Britain.

6. There are also various legends of medieval origin about cities that sank underground or into the sea because of some collective sin committed by the inhabitants. These towns return to earth every hundred years for a few hours, only to sink back to their eternal existence in perpetual limbo.

Marvelous objects

There are a wide variety of legends describing special objects that are enchanted and seem in some ways to possess a soul. A person who owns such an object has great luck, but when it is lost or stolen, all good fortune disappears. The story of Aladdin's lamp is one of the more famous stories of this class. In literature, Tolkien's ring also echoes the motif in oral tradition of a marvelous object.

Miscellaneous legendary creatures

There are other supernatural beings who figure in legends of various sorts. Some of these are reminiscent of the owners of nature or of soul beliefs, but they do not properly fit into those categories.

People frequently ask about dragons, a type of legendary monster that has attracted a great deal of literary attention over the centuries. Folklorists divide creatures of the supernatural into two groups: those that the folk tell stories about encountering (consider how people today may describe evidence of a ghost or of seeing a UFO), and those of a distant time. Dragons, like giants, tended to be confined to a remote past. They were believed to exist, but people were not likely to think they still existed or that anyone would realistically encounter one. So, people thought stories of dragon slayings and of great heroes including St. George, were true, but they belonged to a former time or in some far-off, inaccessible location. The dividing line in the mind of the folk is whether one was likely to encounter a dragon in one's lifetime, and the answer for the most part in Europe was no. The folk believed they once existed; they told many stories of how heroes encountered and killed them, and those heroes may have seemed quite near historically, but the type of heroics they exhibited – the killing of a dragon or of a giant – was simply not something the folk who told those stories thought could occur in their own lifetime in their own village. And that is what separates the belief in dragons from, for example, the way the folk regarded elves, fairies, and *huldre* of Northern Europe.

The supernatural creatures in the pantheon of a culture can and often do figure in both legends and folktales, but the nature of the story determines whether the audience is to believe the account, and the folktale emancipates the supernatural creatures as much as it does the human players to do fantastic things. Giants and dragons, like elves, fairies, and *huldrefolk*, figured in both legends and folktales in Northern Europe. In legends, giants and dragons feature in stories about the past that might explain an aspect of the landscape or something that occurred in a former time. They also figured in folktales in a fantastic setting, untethered to the real world because of the fictional nature of the genre.

There are medieval examples of texts claiming to see fiery dragons in atmospheric or astronomical events. These are typically expressions of literacy, so it is only possible to speculate about how the illiterate peasantry viewed the phenomena. Assuming for a moment that medieval peasants concurred that the incidents were expressions of dragons, the phenomenon was still a step removed from encountering the creatures because of the distance involved. In the body of ethnographic literature based on the work of folklorists in the nineteenth and twentieth centuries, one can find records of conversations with people who really believed they had encountered elves, fairies, *huldre*, and trolls. The same is true of ghosts, which continues to thrive in both Europe and North America. These are very real encounters for believers, but one does not see anything on this level when it comes to dragons or giants. Folklorists make that distinction in part because the folk recognize a similar difference.

Elsewhere in the world, there may be people who believe they have encountered all sorts of monsters. English speakers sometimes apply the word "dragon" to describe creatures in foreign lands, but that does not mean the folklore in question is historically linked to the classic European dragon, which has had such a profound effect on everything from folktales and legends to fantasy literature. This species of extraordinary creature was acknowledged to have existed by the pre-modern folk of Northern Europe, but only in a remote time.

Finally, regarding unicorns: it is important to point out that folk legends about miraculous horses with a single horn do not generally exist. The European peasantry simply did not believe in them and did not tell stories about encounters with them. They told stories about encountering fairies, mermaids (or seal people), and trolls, and they told about the past existence of creatures such as giants and dragons. But unicorns are virtually absent from material gathered from the folk.

The unicorn was an abstraction of the intelligentsia. While many fantastic creatures that appear in literature drew inspiration from the illiterate folk, a few like the unicorn were strictly literary (one often encounters exotic beasts in medieval bestiaries, but many were not popularly seen to exist by the peasantry). Obviously reports of sightings of creatures in exotic settings that seemed like unicorns or the importation of a narwhal tusk could serve to confirm the existence of unicorns, but this would have been something entertained at court, not normally in the village.

CHAPTER 10 CHRISTIANIZATION, INDUSTRIALIZATION, AND IMMIGRATION

European folklore faced two significance barriers in time that caused beliefs and motifs to change in a variety of ways. The first was Christianization. The second was the combined effects of industrialization and immigration.

The earlier analysis of the Lenore story identifies pre-Christian and post-conversion forms of a legend. Similarly, the pagan musician who learns fiddling from the water sprite pays a less profound price than his Christian successor who learns from the devil at the cost of his soul. The introduction of Christianity in Europe and conversion internationally, regardless of the religion, profoundly affected local beliefs and legends. With historical documents, it is possible to examine how this process unfolded, shedding light on the boundary in time, through which oral tradition passed and mutated.

The discussion above mentions the *skogsrå*, the forest sprite who entices hunters and charcoal burners, but her hideous hollow back serves as a sign of her supernatural and dangerous nature. In Germany, she was known as the *Waldfrau*, the forest woman. Minnesingers, the troubadours of Germany, used the motif to describe *Frau Welt* or Dame World, an ideal symbol of the alluring wickedness of the world and its pleasures. Like the *skogsrå*, she was beautiful from the front but had a hideously ugly back.

These two entities draw on a common origin, but *Frau Welt* is the literary Christian world's attempt to incorporate and adapt a folk motif to serve the new religion and ethos. The comparison of recent legendary material with *Lieder*, the songs of medieval minnesingers, creates two difficulties. First there is the problem of stylistic difference between the two sources. The legend is an expression of widespread belief and tradition, whereas the medieval song is the work of a single artist. Care must be taken, then, to distinguish between those parts of the *Lieder* that the artist invented and those that contemporary folklore inspired. The second difficulty arises from the amount of time that separates the Lieder from recent legends. A comparison of nineteenth-century peasant folklore with medieval literature is fully justified, however, because folk culture was extremely conservative. Material collected in the nineteenth century is likely to echo what existed at least as far back as the fifteenth century. In addition, the wide distribution of the idea of the forest sprite reinforces the conclusion that it is an older part of the European folk culture. It is not unreasonable, therefore, to conclude that something like the *Waldfrau* and the *skogsrå* was part of medieval German folklore.

The manifestations of Dame World are by no means restricted to the *Lieder* of the minnesingers. She also appears in the art of the period. Medieval sculptors placed her among the portals of the cathedrals of Worms and Freiburg, for example. Even without consideration of the pre-industrial forest sprite, it is reasonable to infer from the broad distribution of Dame World that a similar motif was also popular in medieval folk culture. Although the statues of Dame World furnish a substantial picture of what the corresponding oral tradition might have described, the poems of the minnesingers provide more details than any other source that deals with this haunting creature of the medieval pantheon.

The poet Walther von der Vogelweide (ca. 1170-ca. 1230), for example, writes that

> When I saw you directly under my eyes
> Then your beauty was revealed, a marvelous thing.
> But the shame was so great.
> When I saw your back,
> That I will evermore scold you.

The ugly and beautiful halves of Dame World and the poet's renunciation of her delights are typical of these songs, repeated, for example, in the Weldsüsse-Lieder" of Neidhart von Reuenthal (ca. 1190-1236/7).

The protagonist in the medieval poems becomes aware that Dame World is treacherous and evil once he sees her hollow back, and thus he is usually able to repent and avoid her snare. The poem "Der Welt Lohn" by Konrad von Würzburg (ca. 1230-1287) breaks with this pattern. Here, a knight is lying on his deathbed when a beautiful maiden approaches him and tells him that she has come to give him his reward for the services that he granted her during his entire life. When he asks who she is, she answers:

> "I am the World!
> "You should look at me from behind:

"See, this is the reward I bring you."
Her back was hollow of flesh.
It was full of toads and worms.
And it stinks like a carrion dog.
Then he cried and said:
"Alas, that my service was ever known to you!"

This poem, although different from the more optimistic works of Walther von der Vogelweide and Neidhart von Reuenthal, underscores the same characteristics of Dame World. After seducing her victims with life-long pleasures, she seeks to claim their souls, condemning them to the foul stench of hell after death. Dame World is treacherous and diabolical. As a personification of the world, she can be delightful, but as Christian dogma maintains, her pleasures are evil at heart and can lead only to eternal damnation.

The legends of Germany and Scandinavia portray the forest sprite as a beautiful supernatural woman who appears before charcoal burners practicing their trade alone in the deep woods. Christiansen loosely classifies this as Migratory Legend 5095, "Fairy Woman Pursues a Man," but the variants of this legend, which are of interest here, can also be seen as part of the tradition of Tale Type 1137, "The Ogre Blinded (Polyphemus)." This story, including the attempted seduction, the discovery of the sprite's hollow back, and the burning of the sprite, is discussed in Chapter 7.

The forest sprite takes part in a variety of additional legends. She can be helpful or mischievous. Despite the diversity of her characteristics and appearances, there are a few consistent features in the legends. She is beautiful, but she has a deformity that leaves no doubt about her supernatural nature. She is dangerous and should be treated with respect and caution. She wishes to entrap men, but the legends that describe her successful attempts show that she only desires a mate, and in fact, the forest sprite makes an excellent and dutiful wife.

There can be little question that Dame World and the forest sprite share common ground. Both are female. Both are beautiful from the front but have a deformity from behind, and the specific motif of the hollow back is shared by those sprites who do not have a tail. Both women attempt to capture the attentions of mortal men, and in the stories describing these attempts, the man usually escapes after seeing the woman's deformity, thereby realizing her true nature. Most of the differences between the two figures are quite slight. Dame World seduces knights in literature, whereas the forest sprite makes advances to lonely charcoal burners and hunters in the legends of the folk. This contrast is a matter of style and audience.

Dame World distracts men so that they neglect their immortal souls while enjoying the pleasures of the world. Dame World is evil. The forest sprite also wants to capture men, and she uses an enchanting front to allure her prospective victims, but her trap is more innocent. She knows nothing of the soul and only wants a mate. While the forest sprite is dangerous, there is no suggestion in the legends that she is evil, and in fact, she is often helpful.

The similarities of Dame World and the forest sprite, then, indicate that they are related in some way. It is likely that the minnesingers were inspired by the contemporary oral tradition when they wrote about Dame World, and it is reasonable to suggest that something like the forest sprite was the source. The principal difference between Dame World and the forest sprite, that one is evil while the other is merely dangerous, reflects the differences between *Lied* and legend, and between the clerical as opposed to the folk world view. An educated elite wrote the *Lieder* for an aristocratic, educated audience. On the other hand, the peasants who told the legends often had no formal education.

The most important contrasting aspect between the two supernatural beings reflected the fact that the peasantry was out of touch with the idea that the world could be divided into good and evil. This concept came from the Middle East with the Bible, which acquired it from ancient Persia. The fact that Dame World is evil, whereas the forest sprite is simply dangerous, reflects the conservatism of the peasants. The dualism of good and evil, which was the property of the educated of medieval Europe, was too foreign to the peasants of Northern Europe – or even for the lower clergy – and so they reacted to it without enthusiasm. This constituted a major obstacle to the long process of Christianization of the peasantry. For the minnesingers, in touch with the more exotic, educated foundations of their religion, it must have seemed rather obvious that the forest sprite, or her medieval German equivalent, was a perfect symbol for the world, enticing and yet fundamentally corrupt and evil as Christian theology viewed the world. This sort of symbolism would no doubt have been lost on the peasantry.

It is common to view European civilization as a synthesis of Classical and Christian worlds with "barbaric" elements thrown in for flavor. Both the peasantry and the learned repeatedly strove to blend the diverse and often conflicting portions of their complicated heritage. Yet the synthesis, as far as the assimilation of the abstractions of good and evil is concerned, was never really achieved before the Industrial Revolution in Northern Europe. A few examples from both medieval and pre-industrial popular culture suffice to demonstrate this.

One of the pressing problems for the European peasant was how to account for the world's various supernatural beings, entities not mentioned in Christian documents. The folk constantly faced the question of how these creatures fit into the system of the saved and the damned. Educated priests told people, after all, that the strict division between good and evil had universal application. How, then, did the elves and fairies rank in the Divine plan? The peasant was never sure how to answer this question. The educated elite, on the other hand, had no trouble with this problem: since elves and fairies were not mentioned in the Bible as affiliated with God, they were, consequently, evil. This is the position that the Beowulf-poet took in the ninth century when he suggested that elves, like the monster Grendel, descended from Cain.

> From him the evil brood were all born,
> Giants and elves and evil spirits,
> And also the giants who fought against God
> For a long time; He paid them retribution for that.

This sort of interpretation, however, never caught on with the peasantry although it was acceptable to the higher clergy. Many people were condemned as witches for innocently making sacrifices to elves and similar supernatural beings.

Pre-industrial European legends show that peasants until recently thought of elves and fairies as neutral beings, without a definite place in God's spiritually-dichotomized world. Some legends explain that the elves and fairies were angels who refused to take either side in the great conflict between God and Satan. Other legends suggest these supernatural beings were the souls of pre-Christian people, or that they were the deceased who were not good enough for heaven, but not bad enough for hell.

When the peasants did take a stand concerning the position of elves and fairies in relation to God, they generally said that the entities have at least a chance for salvation. Christiansen classifies the stories along this line as Migratory Legend 5050, "The Fairies' Prospect of Salvation." In this legend, someone hears the fairies singing in their mound, and he tells them that they should not be so happy because they have no more chance for salvation than his cane does of sprouting leaves. At this, the music stops, and the fairies begin to weep. When the man awakens the next morning, he finds that his cane has sprouted leaves, and so he hurries back to the mound to tell the fairies that God has sent a sign that they can indeed gain admittance into Heaven. Upon hearing this, the fairies resume their music.

This popular legend shows clearly that if pressed to make a definite judgment, peasants said that the fairies are like men: they are neither good nor evil, and they can attain salvation. The peasants retained a belief in the neutrality of the fairies and at the same time worked them into the Christian cosmology. Here, the synthesis of the Christian concept of good and evil has been tenuously reached. Variants of the legend even incorporate the Biblical motif of the sprouting cane, a sign that told the Jews that the house of Levi was to be the house of priests. The ultimate failure of the peasants' attempt to find a synthesis between the concepts of good and evil and their belief in fairies is indicated by two factors. First, the educated elite of Europe and the higher clergy never accepted this judgment, and second, other legends of the peasantry continued to place the fairies in an ambiguous position in relation to good and evil. In fact, still other legends tell of the fairies' fear of crosses and holy words or how they were driven away by church bells.

The example of the fairy shows how difficult it was for European peasants to place one of their neutral, pre-Christian beliefs into the Christian universe. The treatment of the devil in European folklore illustrates the obstacle peasants faced when assimilating even the most absolute symbol of evil into their belief system. The devil usually appears in the place of the stupid ogre or in the role of a trickster. Although these beings are often the opponents of humanity, and they are certainly dangerous, they are also rather amusing and can be beaten. Peasants clearly understood that the devil wishes to gain human souls, but they could not help thinking of the devil as just one of many perilous supernatural beings in the world. The pre-industrial folklore of Europe shows the devil as an easily-defeated, sometimes rather pathetic creature who was not as evil as Christian dogma taught.

The attempt to find a synthesis between pre-conversion European culture and Christianity was a process that involved all levels of society. A charming example of this occurs in the Inquisition Register of Jacques Fournier, a document that Emmanuel LeRoy Ladurie made famous in his book *Montaillou: The Promised Land of Error* (1979). The fourteenth-century register records a story told by Philippe d'Alayrac of Coustaussa in the French Pyrenees. The excerpt refers to "believers," members of the Albigensian heresy, a movement outlawed by Rome. The tale unfolds as follows:

> Once upon a time, two believers found themselves close to a river. One of them fell asleep. The other stayed awake, and from the mouth of the sleeper he saw emerge a creature like a lizard. Suddenly the lizard, using a plank (or was it a straw?), which stretched from one bank to the other, crossed the river. On the other bank there was a fleshless skull of an ass. And the lizard ran in and out of the openings of the skull. Then it came back over the plank and re-entered the sleeper's mouth. It did that once or twice. Seeing which, the man who was awake thought of a trick: he waited until the lizard was on the other side of the river and approaching the ass's skull.

And then he took away the plank! The lizard left the ass's head and returned to the bank. But he could not get across! The plank was gone! Then the body of the sleeper began to thrash about, but it was unable to wake, despite the efforts of the watcher to arouse it from its sleep. Finally the watcher put the plank across the river. Then the lizard was able to get back and re-enter the body of the sleeper through the mouth. The sleeper immediately awoke, and he told his friend the dream he had just had.

'I dreamed,' he said, 'that I was crossing a river on a plank; then I went into a great palace with many towers and rooms, and when I wanted to come back to the place from which I had set out, there was no plank! I could not get across: I would have been drowned in the river. That was why I thrashed about (in my sleep). Until the plank was put back again and I could return.

The two believers wondered greatly at this adventure, and went and told it to a parfait [a heretical priest], who gave them the key to the mystery: the soul, he told them, remains in a man's body all the time; but a man's spirit or mind goes in and out, just like lizard which went from the sleeper's mouth to the ass's head and vice versa.

This story is a variant of a popular European legend commonly called "The Guntram Legend" after its oldest recorded example, which appears in the "History of the Longobards" of Paul the Deacon (d. 790). Christiansen classifies the story as Migratory Legend 4000, "The Soul of a Sleeping Person Wanders on its Own." For the most part, the tale of Philippe d'Alayrac is an unexceptional variant of this legend. The interpretation that the parfait provides, however, is unique. He explains the legend as a testimonial to the existence of the duality of the soul, a concept that suited his heretical purposes. For most of the peasantry, the ancient legend was simply a testimony to the belief that the soul can occasionally leave the body, and when it does, it assumes the form of an animal. The parfait was trying to reconcile two conflicting traditions – his form of Christianity and the pre-conversion legend.

The peasants must have been frustrated at times when seeking to find a place for their pre-Christian beliefs in the Christian cosmology. Many of these attempts were likely failures, causing the pagan tradition either to die out or to live on in a tenuous way. For example, although the European peasants knew of no reason to reject the Christian abstraction of good and evil, they could never assimilate it completely, and the concept continually conflicted in subtle ways with many of the beliefs that survived conversion. European civilization does not always represent the synthesis of different cultures but rather an uneasy co-existence.

There is at least one example of the successful incorporation of the idea of good and evil into the traditions of the peasantry. This occurs in the legend of the land dead and the sea dead. In this story, a young man walking along the coast at night insults the ghosts of the sea who begin to chase him. The frightened fellow flees through a churchyard and, hurrying past the graves, he cries out, "Up, up, every Christian soul, and save me!" He hears a tremendous noise behind him as he runs to his home. The following morning, the townspeople find jellyfish, sea tangle, and boards from coffins strewn about the churchyard. They conclude that the ghosts of the churchyard must have fought with the sea dead to protect the young man.

Christiansen classifies this story as Migratory Legend 4065, "Ghosts from the Land Fight Ghosts from the Sea." The story serves as an example of peasants applying the Christian dichotomy between good and evil: the dead who are buried in consecrated church ground are helpful and good, while those who were lost at sea without burial rites are outside Christianity and are, therefore, evil. An early variant of the legend illustrates that this was not the original point of view.

The thirteenth-century Icelandic *Eyrbyggia Saga* includes an episode that is strongly reminiscent of Legend 4065. A series of illnesses left several people dead and buried, but their animated corpses began to haunt a certain farm. Shortly after this, a ship from the same farm was lost at sea and five sailors were never found. The household had a funeral feast for the lost men. No sooner were the people seated then the dead sailors entered the room, leaving seaweed and puddles of seawater wherever they went. The corpses warmed themselves by the fire. They returned each night, even after the funeral feasts had ended, but now even more dead people arrived, these covered with dirt, which they shook off and threw at the dead from the sea. The two groups, those buried on land and those lost at sea, met each night and quarreled until the owner of the household charged them with trespassing, at which the corpses left for good.

This early variant of Legend 4065 lacks a Christian point of view. Both groups of dead are equally troublesome, and neither has assumed a good or evil role although they are clearly antagonistic to one another, anticipating the later legend. Since recent variants of the legend exhibit the Christian dichotomy of the spiritual world, it seems likely that peasants modified Legend 4065 sometime after conversion. Although the legend is an example of the successful integration of the concept of good and evil, it is the exception and not the rule.

Dame World represents an attempt on the part of the medieval German minnesingers to Christianize a popular belief in something like the forest sprite. By making her a symbol of the evil of the world, these troubadours underscored the pressing dilemma that faced the medieval peasant. Many folk beliefs did not fit into the Christian cosmology and yet the peasants were not willing to forsake Christianity. If Dame World had diffused back into the popular culture and had replaced her pre-conversion counterpart, this one motif, at least, would have reached a complete synthesis between the Christian and pre-conversion beliefs. This did not happen, however, and the forest sprite lived on in recent folklore, dangerous but amoral.

Other beliefs and legends were affected more directly by Christianization. Conflict between the land dead and the sea dead resulted in people perceiving one as Christian, and therefore good, and the other as unconsecrated or non-Christian, and therefore evil, at least in the sense that it struggled with and was perhaps envious of the sanctified dead buried in consecrated ground. The Lenore legend shed its former message about devotion to one's husband as being more important than life; conversion successfully changed this story as well. In the case of the legend about the soul of the sleeper existing in the form of an animal, the idea was perhaps too far from the realm of Christianity to allow the new religion to lay claim to it. The legend persisted, but it was generally unaffected by the new religion.

Christianization represents a significant boundary in the history of folklore. Similarly, conversions to other religions affected oral traditions elsewhere. The indigenous Tibetan Bon religion was forced to accommodate the introduction of Buddhism. The same was true of the Japanese Shinto faith. In each of these cases, much of the pre-conversion traditions survived, provided there was sufficient flexibility to mold the local folklore around the new religion.

Industrialization and immigration represented yet another important barrier for folklore, but this transition resulted in the extinction of much of the earlier traditions. Changes associated with the transformation caused a steady shift from rural to urban and illiterate to literate. Ultimately, it has led to a population that increasingly adheres to an analytical worldview. Cornish legends and beliefs associated with the underground knocker, a spirit of the mines, provides an example of how these two forces – industrialization and immigration – affected oral tradition.

The knockers, also known as buccas, were small supernatural miners who worked in old drifts or sometimes in proximity of human tin miners. They were male, reflecting the pre-industrial restraint in Cornish culture, which only allowed men to work underground. The knockers were known to rap on timbers to warn of danger. They were also described as leading miners of good character to ore bodies, while also punishing disrespectful or otherwise ill-tempered miners. They were, in short, dangerous but also helpful, depending on the nature of the miner.

Before industrialization, Cornish mining normally consisted of what was called tribute work. This approach allowed for a miner or a small group of miners to contract with a land owner. The miners could then extract as much tin as possible over a set period. Profit was predicated on the hard work of the miner, but also on a bit of luck, so pre-industrial folklore included the idea that underground rapping could lead miners to better ore bodies.

With industrialization, Cornish mining shifted: miners became wage earners in large-scale mining. The value of ore discovered was of less concern because miners earned their salaries on time spent rather than on the value of ore retrieved. Safety continued to be a concern, so the idea of a supernatural being warning of dangers remained a viable part of Cornish folklore. Punishing disrespectful miners was also consistent with the industrial environment, so those stories also survived.

Generally, immigration caused the extinction of beliefs in fairy-type supernatural beings, if not at first, then almost always with the following generation. Throughout Britain and Ireland, there has been a long-standing tendency to blur the distinction between ghosts and fairies, so it is not surprising that knockers were often referred to as the ghosts of ancient miners. But their conduct and the descriptions of their appearance link them clearly to the world of the fairy and elf. It is surprising that the Cornish knocker not only survived immigration, but that it also thrived in its new homes in the American West, at times being adopted by non-Cornish miners. The "Tommyknocker," as the supernatural being was typically called in North America, seemed even more like a ghost, and they were often referred to as the spirits of miners who had died in the mine. At the same time, the Tommyknocker often retained its elf-like appearance and mischievous nature. New World stories emphasized the role of the Tommyknocker in warning of danger while its role in punishing poorly-behaved miners was rarer.

These two historical events – industrialization and immigration – had profound effects on the traditions about the Cornish knocker. The belief survived, but it was affected. And while stories in Cornwall all but disappeared by the early twentieth century, it was possible to hear about Tommyknockers in the American West as late as the 1950s. As previously discussed, Carl Wilhelm von Sydow introduced the idea of geographic zones that caused diffusing traditions to mutate, referring to the variants as "ecotypes." This same process, then, can also be applied to traditions as they diffuse through time. Just as the beliefs in one area would require an imported tradition to change if it brought with it ideas that were incompatible with its new home, historical periods can see differences in belief and culture that affect traditions. Perhaps many more examples can be described in a similar manner.

One aspect of folklore affected by industrialization has been the subject of widespread exploitation in modern literature. Initially fairies featured prominently in publications and retained their original power. Shakespeare frequently employed supernatural beings of nature, but his audience was filled with believers, so he had to employ the subject with caution. At the end of "A Midsummer Night's Dream," the elf known as Puck apologizes to the audience for taunting dangerous supernatural powers with their prominent display on stage. Shakespeare's apology to the audience – and to the supernatural – was an attempt to set things back to order so people would not leave horrified that they may have treaded on hazardous ground. Puck's farewell speech reads as follows.

If we shadows have offended,
Think but this, and all is mended –
That you have slumb'red here
While these visions did appear.
And this weak and idle theme,
No more yielding but a dream,
Gentles, do not reprehend.
And, as I am an honest Puck,
If we have unearned luck
Now to 'scape the serpents tongue,
We will make amends ere long;
Else the Puck a liar call.
So, good night unto you all.
Give me your hands, if we be friends,
And Robin shall restore amends.

Later in the seventeenth century, Robert Kirk of Scotland (1644-1697) published his book, *The Secret Commonwealth of Elves, Fauns and Fairies*. Kirk was attempting to define the realm of the supernatural for a changing world. He was clearly convinced that these hidden creatures existed and that people's fading beliefs placed them in danger as they might happen to treat the realm with less respect.

Irishman William Allingham (1824-1889) published his poem, "The Fairies," in 1883, perhaps not out of belief, but clearly his composition was grounded upon respect for the tradition. His is a reasonably faithful depiction of the fairy world, which by the late nineteenth century still retained much of its original power. The poet used motifs well known in his contemporary folklore, but a "cute" element has crept in, a harbinger of future things.

For much of the literate world, the modern elf has descended into the realm of childish things, becoming charming, diminutive, and generally harmless. This representation is far removed from the original inspiration, which was capable of manifesting as a human-sized, powerful entity to be feared and respected. The ability of fairies to fly was due to magical ability to transcend the laws of nature, not because they had wings. Their modern literary counterpart, outfitted with insect wings, flitted about on missions largely irrelevant to adults. For over one hundred years, illustrators and authors have exploited the motifs, but they have participated in a transformation that deprives the supernatural beings of their original power. Wil Huygen and Rien Portvliet's *Gnomes* (1977) delves into the subject extensively, but without belief, the danger and magic have dissipated. Wings are noticeably absent, but their depiction remains childlike.

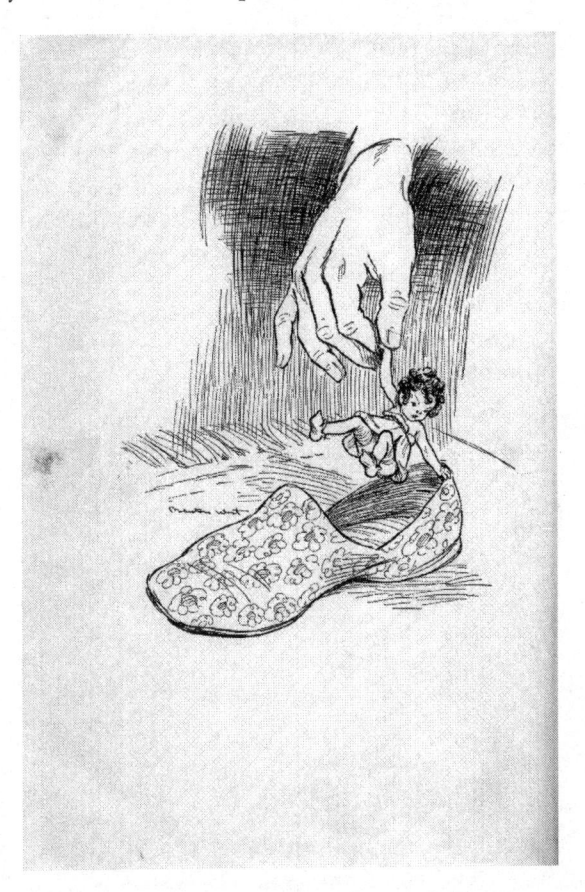

Figure 12. Anne Pérez-Guerra's *Poppy or the Adventures of a Fairy* (1931) features illustrations by Benton West. The story is about Poppy, "a fairy, a four-inch fairy, who had lost her way in the World of People." Although she too lacks wings, Poppy is an example of the evolution from powerful supernatural being to darling of children's literature.

With industrialization and immigration, folklore passed through two profoundly important bottlenecks, and much was lost. The disruption of oral traditions inspired a century or more of frantic collection of beliefs and stories before they were gone forever. Surviving traditions, often in mutated form, represent only a small fraction of what existed before, but even survival did not guarantee immortality. Remnants of peasant folklore continue to disappear with every generation.

Despite what may at times seem to be the total extinction of the old beliefs, some things seem apt to survive. The recently appearing book by Marjorie T. Johnson, *Seeing Fairies: From the Lost Archives of the Fairy Investigation Society, Authentic Reports of Fairies in Modern Times* (2014) demonstrates that at least for some people, the idea that fairies are real remains a viable tradition. Whether drawing from the past or crafting something new for the future, humanity will not be deprived of its folklore. Industrialization did not create a sterile zone for folk belief and story. Modernization may have extinguished and altered older traditions, but a dynamic environment emerged that fostered new types of folklore. This modern counterpart of peasant tradition is often called urban folklore.

Chapter 11 Urban Folklore and the Most Recent Chapter

Like the peasant stories that preceded it, urban folklore offers life-saving information. It tells us when to be cautious about handling cereal boxes at the store because a clerk has Hantavirus and is spreading it by handling groceries. It tells us to stop that unseemly, greedy practice of checking coin returns in vending machines. It seems that evil, drug-using AIDS patients are leaving their infected needles in the returns with the hope of spreading disease throughout America – or at least among the greedy. And it warns us away from eating bananas because some have been found to be covered with flesh-eating bacteria from South and Central America.

Of course, none of these helpful hints have been found to be based on anything that is true. Between investigations by www.snopes.com and the Centers for Disease Control and Prevention, one urban legend after the next has been proven to be false. But these and hundreds of other tales make for great stories, and people will always have a thirst for this sort of thing. There are also several newer forms of folklore that have emerged in modern North American and European culture. The following is an overview of various forms that is not inclusive, nor can it hope to be up-to-date since modern folklore consists of a dynamic well of creativity that continually spawns new stories that circulate rapidly.

Gremlins and UFOs

Pilots during World War II described a series of unusual apparitions that people sometimes jokingly said were supernatural. They called phantom lights in the sky "foo-fighters," and disappearing tools and quirky failures of machines became the work of "gremlins," although the latter date to at least the 1920s. The unusual circumstance of some of these phenomena attracted attention. In the mid to late twentieth century, the sightings of UFOs – "Unidentified Flying Objects" – became common, and they have also become part of folklore.

After the war, interpretations of odd things in the sky focused on terrestrial technological explanations, but beginning in the early 1950s aviator and author Donald Keyhoe (1897-1988) began writing about the idea that these atmospheric sights were, in fact, evidence of alien visits. Perhaps following the lead of literature, the belief in alien visitors became a cornerstone of modern North American folklore. As has happened for centuries, the interplay of literature and oral tradition continues. While the belief in these creatures is widespread internationally, it was not universal. In 1982, I was interviewing an Irish woman who had seen banshees and believed resolutely in the fairies of Ireland. When I asked if she believed in UFOs, she answered, "Oh, that's what you Americans believe." She then laughed derisively.

In fact, aliens have taken the place, in many respects, of the supernatural beings of nature. The modern "little green men" abduct people, fly around in the night, and leave rings in fields. The similarities shared by elves and aliens could be the result of two causes. They are either due to transference of older motifs to the newer idea of aliens, or they are a new interpretation applied to similar, unusual phenomena, resulting in a parallel tradition. Both factors may be present at the same time.

People often apply extraordinary explanations to things that are not easily understood. If a person believes in elves, then the rush of something unusual across the night sky, a brown circle in a field, or the unexplained disappearance of someone can all be attributed to the supernatural owners of nature. Even as the modern, technological, literate society extinguishes the belief in fairies, it simultaneously opens the door to the idea of space flight; people in this modern world can imagine extraordinary travelers whose abilities make them nearly supernatural. It is easy, consequently, to look to aliens to explain astonishing things that seem beyond our ability to comprehend with more normal explanations.

Urban Legends

Utah folklorist Jan Harold Brunvand (1933-) has published several books on urban legends, raising the subject to a level of awareness that it had not previously enjoyed. The media frequently publishes these stories as true, but now the Internet often reproduces them as well. At the same time, debunking websites seek to extinguish the fires of urban legends, resulting in an ebb and flow of folklore, creation and spread followed by debunking and retreat. Nevertheless, the urban legend is most at home as a truly oral form of folklore. People tell the stories to be believed just like their legendary predecessors.

Urban legends include a range of information on many subjects including live animals and microwaves, the dangers of beehive hairdos, the hazards of adolescent dating (particularly when homicidal maniacs escape from local mental institutions), and the possibility of becoming an unwilling organ donor while on vacation. This is clearly important information! With the internet, stories are often short-lived, in part because of debunkers in the media and on the Internet, but also because many urban legends describe new technologies or passing fashions. Thus, having poisonous spiders nesting in a sprayed-and-seldom-washed beehive hairdo would only be appropriate when that style was in vogue. Similarly, people born after 1975 are less likely to have heard the story of the old woman who thought it would be a good idea to dry her newly-washed poodle in the microwave: the story could only thrive when microwaves represented new technology, with all the angst that sort of thing can produce.

One of the most persistent forms of urban folklore involves legends about ghosts. Some, such as the well-known "Vanishing Hitchhiker," are clearly urban legends of the sort that Brunvand collects, but in this case, the story appears to have pre-modern roots. The most common legends dealing with ghosts in general are what von Sydow would call memorates. These are personal recollections that families tell of their own histories about departed loved ones. There has been little collection of these stories because each example is so specific to the individual circumstance. Like the material related to traditional European folklore, it is possible to recognize that while the memorates may not be traditional, the beliefs behind them and the conventions of telling them are. This topic remains a fertile opportunity for research.

Because of various factors, Urban Legends can come and go quickly. As a genre, they are reminiscent of the pre-industrial Migratory Legends, but those stories lasted for decades if not centuries, while an Urban Legend can have a much briefer life span. Fortunately, the folk are extremely creative and new legends emerge to take the place of those that society has discarded. Keeping up with the constantly changing spectrum of stories makes folklore collection and analysis a challenge. Brunvand remains the best source on this genre of folklore.

Conspiracy Theories

Urban Legends often have a light, humorous tone, but for at least one group of these stories, this is not the case. North America has provided fertile soil for the growth of conspiracy theories, although their popularity has increasingly become international. This is a specialized form of Urban

Legend, usually involving the government as the central motif. These stories maintain that the U.S. government, or a select group of people within the government, conspires to achieve something or to withhold evidence about something.

According to cycles within this genre, Franklin Delano Roosevelt knew about but purposely did not act on the Japanese attack on Pearl Harbor in 1941. The government withholds evidence of alien landings on earth, and Nevada's Area 51 preserves physical evidence of these points of contact, including alien bodies from crash sites. Many people believe that the 1963 assassination of President John F. Kennedy was a government conspiracy, if not in the actual act, then in the covering up of the truth. The same is purported to be true regarding the attack on the Twin Towers in New York on September 11, 2001.

Occasionally, specific groups believe there is a conspiracy related to themselves: some Native Americans maintain that genetic testing of various groups internationally is part of an effort to produce viruses that will only kill disenfranchised minorities and members of the Third World. Similarly, in the early 1990s, some Egyptians refused to use shampoo made in Israel because of the belief that the Jewish state was using these exports to hurt followers of Islam. The folk tradition maintained that the shampoo contained chemicals that would make their hair fall out. (This was discussed on "All Things Considered," National Public Radio, October 20, 2000.)

Xerox Lore

Before the Internet, copies of humorous illustrations circulated throughout North America, although distribution from hand to hand was sluggish compared with its modern Internet counterpart. Even though the Internet has taken over much of the market for this sort of thing, hardcopies of certain cartoons remain standards at the office. University of California, Berkeley folklorist, Alan Dundes and attorney, Carl R. Pagter, pioneered the subject with the publication of their book, *Work Hard and You Shall Be Rewarded: Urban Folklore from the Paperwork Empire* (1975). Subsequently, Pagter and Dundes published three additional books on the subject. Their material is often racist and/or sexist, and it frequently has a sexual content not appropriate for certain parts of society.

Dundes had to overcome an initial criticism regarding whether the commonly circulated photocopy was folklore. His introduction to *Work Hard and You Shall Be Rewarded* includes a lengthy defense about why this must be thought of as a form of folklore. He argues that the term "folk" can no longer refer, exclusively, the illiterate peasants, since the mass of society is now literate. The second problem Dundes addresses is the definition of the word "lore." Conservative folklorists have defined the term to describe material transmitted orally. Dundes was convinced that this was no longer applicable and that when the folk circulate something like the cartoons and written documents with frequency, the material must be regarded as lore. There can be little question that many of these cartoons are traditional, and in our post-modern environment, we are forced to reassess numerous assumptions previously held about folklore.

The problem comes down to organization and meaning. Dundes describes how each type of cartoon and written document reflects an aspect of American society. Arriving at a comprehensive way to treat the material is still needed.

Figure 13. "Before 6 Beers/After 6 Beers": The modern folk of North America have enjoyed photocopied cartoons such as this for years, making it a staple of the work place. Folklorist Alan Dundes called this sort of illustration Xerox lore. This illustration, however, was collected from the Internet in October 2000, demonstrating the close relationship of the two forms of media.

Web Lore

The Internet has introduced a new means to distribute what was once exclusively printed folklore, and the web has affected the way this genre of tradition develops and diffuses. It is now possible for the entire world to consume humorous cartoons and writing very quickly. All sorts of things can be altered and transmitted internationally in a matter of minutes. The Web allows an immediate response from the folk, creating and disposing of traditions within days. Web humor is easily run off, copied, and introduced to the realm of Xerox lore to which it is closely related. In fact, questions and issues raised about Xerox lore generally apply to Web lore, but now, the very meaning of "folk" is challenged in a new way. With this genre, the term can be defined in transnational terms.

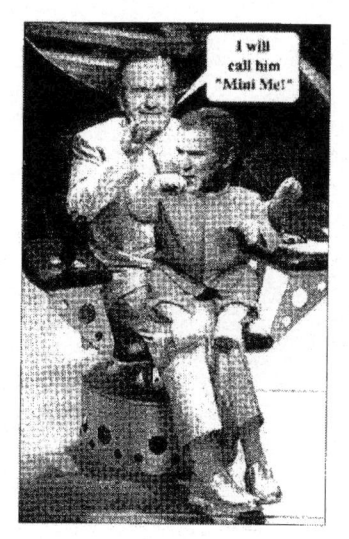

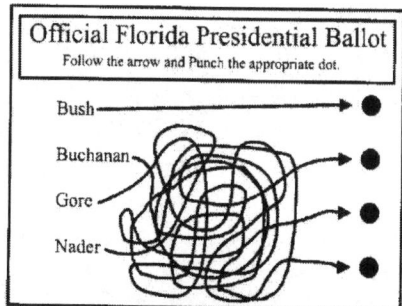

Figure 14. Three forms of campaign humor from the Internet. Two are partisan (one each for Gore and Bush) and one tends to be more bipartisan. These appeared on the Internet within days of the election of November 2000. There are thousands of examples from the campaign and election, but there is no question that November 7, 2000 gave the nation a revived interest in political humor. The "Official Florida Presidential Ballot," collected on November 9, 2000 floated between Web and Xerox lore.

The explosive and immediate potential of Web lore was demonstrated early on by the response to the 2000 presidential campaign between George

W. Bush and Al Gore. Gore won more popular votes than Bush, but Bush claimed to have won more electoral votes, particularly in the hotly contested Florida race, resulting in legal questions and challenges. Even before the election, humorous expositions and cartoons began to appear on the Internet. These were both partisan and bi-partisan.

The campaign was one thing, but even the collective wisdom of the folk could not anticipate what would happen with the ambiguous results of the election. A new chapter of material appeared on the Web immediately after Election Day. One form was especially open to modification and elaboration by the folk. Shortly after November 7, a simple notice of "Revocation of Independence from the Queen of England" appeared on various Internet sites. This letter included four simple demands associated with revocation: Look up "revoke" in a dictionary; Learn at least the first four lines of "God Save the Queen"; Start referring to "soccer" as football; Declare war on Quebec.

Within days, the folk had expanded the demands. There were soon ten or more requirements placed on the new North American subjects of the Queen. Older conditions became more elaborate. Different versions appeared, indicating that people were modifying them as they transmitted the document. Finally, a reply to the revocation appeared on the Internet, as insulting to the United Kingdom as the first letters had been to the United States. The response of media comedians to the election paralleled this Internet chatter, but the folk were not to be outdone. The combination of Internet and copying machines provided the people with all they needed to demonstrate that they know an opportunity for a joke when they see one. This is only one example of an enormously popular, well-used venue for creative expression. And it has become only more exploited since the election of 2000.

A more recent aspect of Web lore is made possible by improved computer graphics in the twenty-first century: the Internet meme employs a well-known image, exchanging the caption with various witticisms. Repeated use of a single image makes the result a traditional cultural practice. The fact that the best captions are then exchanged and sent around the world makes them tradition on another level. It is a new form of folklore, a subgenre of Web lore.

In all, the various forms of contemporary folklore are reassuring. They clearly indicate that folklore is alive and well in the modern environment. Disruptive changes over the past two hundred years have extinguished life styles and vast amounts of oral tradition, customs, and beliefs, but the folk are tenacious. People will create folklore, no matter the circumstance.

Figure 15. Internet memes are created and distributed. Because they reuse a set background image, they are in a sense traditional as is the genre in general.

American psychologist Walter Fisher (b. 1931) has proposed with his "narrative paradigm" that people tell stories because the device is essential to human communication. He suggests that this aspect of our species is sufficiently significant that we should be referred to as "Homo narrans." The degree to which this idea is valid may be open to debate, but the observation – that storytelling is indispensable to people – is at the heart of why there will always be folklore.

Two challenges face the folklorist of the twenty-first century. First, there are still many questions about extinct forms of folklore that deserve answers. In the twenty-first century, we are generally deprived of the opportunity to talk to active pre-modern tradition bearers to gain perspective. Work on these subjects will increasingly be restricted to archives, and yet the material, so diligently collected for over one hundred years, represents an open door to the further understanding of the nature of folklore.

The second challenge involves identifying, recording, ordering, and understanding the new forms of folklore that spontaneously come into existence in a post-modern environment. The good news is that the folk will always provide employment security for folklorists. Every day, there is something new to study.

APPENDIX 1 FOLKLORE AND NATIONALISM

Modern professional folklore collecting began in Europe in the early nineteenth century. Whether by coincidence or cause, this was also a time when nationalism was in vogue in Europe. Johann Gottfried Herder (1744-1803) played a critical role in the history of folklore studies and nationalism. He called for Germans and others to strive for nationhood and to use language and popular traditions to reinforce and inspire national cultures and consciousness. With the assertion that this material is important, Herder broke with Enlightenment thinkers who stressed the universal shared aspects of humanity rather than the cultural characteristics that divided people. In the Germanies, scholars such as Johann Gottlieb Fichte (1762-1814) and the poets Clemens Brentano (1778-1842) and Achim von Arnim (1781-1831) answered Herder's call.

Fichte was a professor at the University of Berlin during Napoleon's occupation of the German states. He feared that German culture and language might become extinct because of the oppressive domination of the French. In his "Addresses to the German Nation," public lectures held in 1807 and 1808, Fichte attempted to alert Germans to this possibility. Echoing Herder, he stressed the idea that language held the identity of a culture, a people, and a nation, and that language shaped a nation's destiny and helped define its unique qualities.

The work of Brentano and von Arnim drew on popular traditions for inspiration and material, but they were removed from the modern notion of professional collection of folklore. Instead, they saw little reason to remain true to their sources: for them, the most important goal was to create a national literature in the vernacular language, which would foster German awareness and inspire a generation of patriots.

During the early nineteenth century, when an increasing number of people were becoming aware of Herder's message, Jacob and Wilhelm Grimm approached popular tradition in a new way. The brothers had studied under Friedrich Karl von Savigny (1779-1861), who stressed precise historical method to arrive at a better understanding of German heritage. Although the sweeping Romanticism of Herder influenced them, the brothers were not content with exploiting popular motifs in literature. Instead, they collected the material in a manner that approached (but did not always reach) modern professional standards.

The work of the Grimm brothers inspired counterparts throughout Europe, particularly where people strove for nationhood. The scholarly tradition of folklore collecting paralleled that of the antiquarians and the "folklore" poets. The effectiveness of each in inspiring nationalism is difficult to evaluate and does not lend itself to simple generalizations. Nevertheless, some conclusions are possible. Early folklorists clearly helped define the nations as they fought for their own sovereignty. The politicians of nations that grew from the independence movements regularly pay homage to these early custodians of the popular culture.

Historian Hans Kohn (1944) suggests that "Herder, who can be regarded as the first representative of German nationalism and of folk nationalism generally, was influenced by Rousseau's stress upon the primitive and pre-civilized stages of human development, the national folkdom of 'unspoiled people.'" He further asserts that "the new emphasis in Germany upon indigenous originality" was also due to a general trend in European thought. He suggests that while the Romantic-era notion of the value of local cultural roots had expression in Britain, many British publications ultimately had a greater effect in Germany. These included Samuel Richardson's "Clarissa" (1748) and "Sir Charles Grandison" (1753), Edward Young's "Night Thoughts" (1742), Thomas Percy's "Reliques of Ancient English Poetry" (1765), and especially the supposed third-century Celtic literature invented by James MacPherson, including *Fragments of Ancient Poetry Collected in the Highlands of Scotland*, *Fingal*, and *The Works of Ossian* (1760-1773). In Germany, these British poets and authors helped inspire the idea that it was more important to study national traditions and originality rather than to consider universal standards and values.

Kohn suggests, however, that Herder was misunderstood and that his intention was not to be nationalistic. Writing in 1944 during the depths of World War II, Kohn noted that "today's German nationalism overlooks that no eighteenth century thinker – not even Herder – regarded the reality of the folk as a natural and therefore unchangeable and unchallengeable foundation of history." Nevertheless, the work of Herder provides an important building block for those who wished to find the justification for nationalism in the folk.

It is within this context that a few poets and antiquarians developed an interest in folk narrative. Brentano and von Arnim exploited German folk traditions as fertile ground for a new national literature. Together, they published a collection of poetry titled *Des Knaben Wunderhorn* (*The Boy with the Wonder Horn*) between 1805 and 1808. Using folk narrative, the two hoped to draw attention to the literary potential of German language and culture with *Kunstmärchen*, a term that can be translated as "art folktales" or more simply, "fairytales." Von Arnim, in particular, worked with the genre of *Kunstmärchen*, developing it as a distinct form of literary fiction. His stories are reminiscent of those of James MacPherson, the author of a widely popular collection of allegedly ancient Scottish writings. MacPherson's "Ossian" poems were later proven to be a hoax, but it was not before he inspired others, including Sir Walter Scott.

The literary tradition of von Arnim and Brentano had a profound influence on the young Grimm brothers. Although the Grimms were students of von Savigny, trained in a strict scholarly historical tradition, they no doubt saw the value of von Arnim's and Brentano's work. In fact, they lent an early manuscript of their *Märchen* collection to Brentano, hoping to collaborate. Although the gesture yielded nothing, it was within this tradition that the German brothers later published their *Kinder und Hausmärchen*. With their volume of collected folktales, the Grimms were in effect creating a new discipline of the humanities by professionally gathering and analyzing oral tradition. Nevertheless, they could not see the historical importance of their small step. Lacking a historical perspective of their early academic triumph, the Grimm brothers indulged in some alteration of the material they collected. They also saw nothing wrong with including folktales from elsewhere that appeared in earlier publications. These were eliminated, for the most part, from subsequent editions, but the brothers still demonstrated a less-than-scholarly stance by modern standards when initially dealing with the material. Their step away from the work of Brentano and von Arnim was smaller at first than later folklorists might prefer to think.

Literature for art's sake, however, was not the only influence on the Grimm brothers. That they were active politically is clear: they participated in the famous movements at Göttinger University in protest of censorship. This led to their dismissal in 1838 as part of the "Göttinger Seven." There is also good evidence that they were extremely interested in German nationalism. Late in his career, Jacob Grimm, for example, wrote, "how often the sad face of our fatherland keeps coming to my mind and makes my heart heavy and my life bitter" (Zipes 1988).

Still, Grimm scholar Jack Zipes (1988) sees the relationship of the brothers to nationalism as extremely complex. He points out that the Grimms were part of a new, growing German bourgeois class. As such, they looked for German unification not simply because of national pride, but also as a means of overthrowing the archaic system of aristocratic domination of the society and economy. Zipes sees the German *Kinder und Hausmärchen*, therefore, as supporting a middle-class point of view as much as a nationalistic one. Of course, the brothers likely wished to see the triumph of both, and they probably hoped their publications would advance those causes.

As historian Theodore S. Hamerow (1969) asserts in his seminal work on German unification, "the achievement of a national unification during the 1860s was a result of the growth of a political consciousness, which had begun only a generation before. In the course of a single lifetime the attitudes of men of education and substance toward public affairs became transformed." It is easy to believe, yet difficult to prove, that the Grimm brothers, as extremely popular authors of the time, were part of this transformation. After all, Hamerow points out that pre-unification Germany was dominated by organizations, which on the surface were not political and yet were part of an effort to "popularize the ideal of unification." Although clearly there were organizations such as the *Nationalverein*, the German National Union, which was overtly political, others such as the Congress of German Economists, the German Commercial Association, professional, athletic, and choral societies, the Association of German Jurists, and the German Society of Sharpshooters were not. Despite this, unification was a frequent theme of their meetings. What could be said of sharpshooters could certainly be extended to more cultural events, particularly during a time when establishing a national identity was of concern. It should come as no surprise that the police watched a meeting of the Main Valley Song Festival because of its nationalist overtones. It is easy to imagine that the publication of *Kinder und Hausmärchen* raised similar concerns with some, and that it was at least as effective as these meetings in creating an atmosphere conducive to nationalism.

It was also within this tradition that Richard Wagner (1813-1883) composed his great operas. In fact, early in his career, he hoped to produce an opera based entirely on the *Märchen* of the Brothers Grimm (Adorno 1984). Ultimately, the study of Germanic myth by Jacob Grimm proved more influential for Wagner: according to the composer's autobiography, *Mein Leben*, he carried a copy of *Teutonic Mythology* wherever he went while composing "Tannhäuser" in 1843. The grander realm of myth rather than the humbler one of *Märchen* was Wagner's setting for his national art form. His use of popular belief, although tapping ancient rather than contemporary material, is in keeping with Brentano and von Arnim: Wagner sought an artistic rather than a scholastically-faithful rendering of myth.

The message of Herder and the example of the Grimm brothers

diffused quickly throughout Europe. Oppressed ethnically-distinct people saw Herder's message as a philosophical justification for achieving national sovereignty. Isolated by the domination of a colonial authority, Iceland provides an example of the effect of nationalism on popular culture. Like the Germanies, Iceland had nationalist-minded people who looked toward the folk for inspiration. In addition, there was an attempt to conserve and publish medieval literature and documents so that the masses could arrive at an understanding of the value of Icelandic national heritage. Coincidentally, the medieval literature itself was based on an earlier attempt to document oral tradition, in part to reinforce nationalism.

Snorri Sturluson (1179-1242), the great writer and antiquarian of medieval Iceland, recorded the island's folk traditions, many of which were slipping away during his lifetime. His *Prose Edda* preserves verses and beliefs that were falling out of favor with the official Icelandic conversion to Christianity in the year 1000. Pagan practices and traditions were fading from memory, and it appears that Snorri realized that if he did not collect the material, it would be lost.

Snorri, however, was a politician, and of more pressing concern in his time was the maneuvering his nation out of the grasp of King Hakon of Norway who sought to fulfill a centuries-old ambition of the Norwegian kings to dominate the free Republic of Iceland to the west. It is difficult to be certain, but it appears that this threat may have contributed to Snorri's desire to record and preserve Icelandic traditions. Snorri's *Heimskringla*, the history of the Norwegian Kings commissioned by King Hakon, can hardly be regarded as royal propaganda. It is relatively even-handed, walking the fence between praise for some kings, condemnation for others, and the history includes a consistent portrayal of the peasants as the honorable fabric of Scandinavian society. Like the *Prose Edda*, it was an attempt to preserve traditions that were vanishing with every new decade. Snorri clearly drew on folk traditions about the remote history of Scandinavia. Folk history depicting the settlers of Iceland as heroes bears a message that could have inspired Snorri's fellow Icelanders to fight for their Republic. It was a theme that apparently inspired King Hakon to demand Snorri's assassination, which occurred in 1242.

Snorri's motives are lost in a past where the history of ideas is not easily traced. He was one of the first Europeans to be seriously interested in the collection of folk traditions, and as a politician, he was probably aware of the ramifications of his scholarship. With the discovery of the New World, the invention of the novel, and the collection of folk traditions, Icelanders have consistently been at the vanguard. Removed from the continental mainstream, however, they had little effect on the rest of Europe, and it was up to other Europeans to rediscover paths trod long before on the tiny island nation.

Appropriately, the nineteenth-century nationalism movement in Iceland worked to preserve the writings of Snorri Sturluson. That medieval scholar had sought to record the traditions of his people. Now his works were considered part of the nation's heritage. Iceland had lost its independence in stages beginning in 1262-1264 with the acceptance of Norwegian royal sovereignty over the island. The 1380 union of Denmark and Norway caused the transfer of the administration of Iceland to Copenhagen.

The idea of nationalism set nineteenth-century Iceland on fire. Jón Sigurdsson (1811-1879) became the most important leader of the Icelandic independence movement. A scholar and politician much like Snorri Sturluson (from whom he was descended), Sigurdsson played a crucial role in the preservation of the medieval manuscripts, editing *Lovsamling for Island*, a collection of Icelandic laws published between 1853 and 1857, and two volumes of *Íslendínga sögur* in 1843 and 1847. In 1843, Sigurdsson negotiated with the Danish king, Christian IX, for the reestablishment of the Althing, the traditional Icelandic parliament, to serve as an advisory council. Agitation along these lines eventually lead to the granting of an Icelandic constitution in 1874, which permitted Iceland to share control of finances and legislation with the Danish crown. In 1903, Denmark granted Iceland a national government, which gained even more autonomy in 1918 when the two nations shared only the monarchy and foreign policy. In 1944, on Sigurdsson's birthday, Iceland severed all ties with Denmark, at the time occupied by the Nazis.

Sigurdsson was an antiquarian who preserved medieval manuscripts with the hope that something of the heart of Icelandic character would survive. His professional counterpart was Jón Arnason (1819-1888) who took his inspiration from the Brothers Grimm and collected material directly from the people. The preface to the 1864 English translation of Arnason's work calls him the "Grimm of Iceland." That same preface asserts that Arnason had been collecting for thirty years, suggesting that he initiated his work in the 1830s, but the exact date of the beginning of the project is unknown. Arnason was the humble but scholarly contemporary of Sigurdsson. He served as librarian of the Reykjavik Cathedral and as secretary to the bishop. His collection was first published in Iceland in 1862 under the title of *Íslenzkar Djoðsögur og Æfintýri*, which Powell and Magnusson translated as "Icelandic National Stories and Tales," but which literally means "Icelandic Legends and Folktales."

Iceland serves as an example of the ramifications of Herder's call for the collection of folk traditions to promote nationalism. This type of interest echoed throughout Europe for much the same reason, and with a similar effect. Herder's philosophical stance combined with the method of the Grimms to inspire folklore collecting wherever ethnic groups sought to define themselves and maintain their traditions.

In Ireland, Patrick Kennedy, Joseph Jacobs, Jeremiah Curtain, D. R. McAnally, Jr., William Butler Yeats, and Lady Gregory all collected and published Irish folklore between 1866 and the turn of the century. Their effort was inspired, not to a small degree, by the desire to preserve the essence of Ireland as it faced the onslaught of English cultural domination. Similarly, the Norwegians used folklore collecting in the nineteenth century to define themselves distinctly from their Danish overlords. The same is true for the Finns, under the domination of the Swedes, the Scots and Welsh under English rule, and the Basque, whose homeland is split between Spain and France.

Of course, there was also folklore collecting in places that did not need a nationalist movement. One of the first collections of folklore was published in France. In the late seventeenth century, Charles Perrault began publishing his *Histoires ou Contes du temps passé*, (*History of Folktales of Past Times*). This seminal work was extremely influential, inspiring von Arnim, Brentano, and the Grimms. Perrault published folktales that many readers still regard as the definitive variants. These include Cinderella, Sleeping Beauty, Bluebeard, and Puss 'n Boots. Many of Perrault's stories were so influential that the Grimms included them in their earlier editions. They later replaced them with German variants, and although the collections of the Grimms are more widely read today than that of Perrault, it is the French versions of these shared tales that invariably serve as the core of popularized stories.

Other countries also embraced the concept of folklore collection, even when a nationalistic movement was not needed. Thus, scholars in Denmark, Sweden, and Russia all began aggressive folklore collecting by the end of the nineteenth century and each has a credible folklore archive.

England presents a different problem. Folklore collecting occurred there, but it largely remained in the hands of antiquarians who gathered material for its own sake without an academic bedrock. These folklorists were not tied to the scholastic flow of ideas and theory that was refining the discipline elsewhere. As a result, there is no single English folklore archives like those in Dublin, Copenhagen, Uppsala, or Berlin. In addition, the English journal *Folklore* spans decades. Its volumes contain tens of thousands of bits of collected material, but there is little in the way of academic observation or philosophical discussion that would link it to the international discipline. That said, the work of Kathryn Briggs and Jacqueline Simpson represents exceptional attempts to place British folklore in the academic mainstream despite its peculiar historical roots.

APPENDIX 2 FOLKLORE, MYTH, AND LITERATURE

The use of folklore in literature predates the interests of von Arnim and Brentano – and even that of Snorri Sturluson, all of whom are described in Appendix 1. *The Epic of Gilgamesh*, nearly four thousand years old, is often regarded as the first book, and it clearly drew on oral tradition. Its incorporation of the story of the flood and the man who survived it is a recognizable type of etiological legend well known from the later Genesis story in the Bible. The use of folktales and legends in literature was a consistent practice throughout history. Homer, Aesop, the Bible, Chaucer, Shakespeare, Boccaccio, the *Arabian Nights*, and the *Gesta Romanorum* all drew on this material.

The influence of von Arnim and Brentano formalized the literary borrowing from folk narrative. From the beginning of the nineteenth century, authors were more self-conscious when using folklore, and the idea of nationalism often served as a philosophical if not political underpinning. The Grimm brothers may have had scientific and academic interests in collecting oral tradition, but Wilhelm, more than Jacob, also sought to produce literature based on or inspired by this material. Others followed in his footsteps, at times straying from the original folklore. The German E. T. A. Hoffman (1776-1822), the Danish author Hans Christian Andersen (1805-1875), and several others experimented with this approach.

By the end of the nineteenth century, much of the original inspiration of Herder, von Arnim, and Brentano was no longer part of the picture. Still, some authors continued to look to folklore as a source of inspiration. The process gave birth to the genre of fantasy literature, but the authors who work in this domain deviate in varying degrees from folklore. The publications of English medievalist J. R. R. Tolkien (1892-1973) are a more recent and noteworthy expression of this literary tradition. He drew directly from older sources to create a world that in many ways reflects the power and form intended by European folklore.

Tolkien's successors have not always claimed such distinction. The best authors to take on the mantle of von Arnim and Brentano understood folklore and folk belief. Though they often strayed from the original inspiration, they were aware of the primary sources, which they typically respected. This cannot be said uniformly of fantasy writers of the late twentieth and early twenty-first centuries, many of whom have only read one another's works, and so they often borrow material, that while once rooted in folk tradition, is far from the realm where it is most at home. The results are worlds of supernatural beings deprived of power, removed from the soil that once spawned belief. The worst of this literature has given birth to a popular view of the fantastic as a place of silly stories and motifs. The original folk literature was a place of power and inspiration.

The use of oral tradition in song has also been a time-honored practice. The history of this process is probably more ancient than its literary parallel. In addition, it has continued to the present day, arguably with less of the contrivance than has occurred in literature. Without the influence of von Arnim and Brentano, songwriters have freely borrowed motifs and stories, continually refreshing the popular repertoire of music.

Appendix 3 The "Real" Events Inspiring Legends

The online subreddit "AskHistorians" – a category of the popular website "reddit.com" – frequently receives questions about how stories originate. A second type of question dances around the issue of whether there were real people or events behind legends, myths, or ancient gods. The following are two responses I provided in 2014 to these sorts of questions.

On the origin of stories:

The answer to this question is somewhere between "we don't know" and "it's just what people do" – that is, they invent these sorts of stories. Several folklorists, including the late Alan Dundes and Jan Harold Brunvand, recognized an opportunity with recent urban legends to finally track down "the source," the point of creation, to better understand how stories originate. For the most part, they were unable to find the point/person of origin to any general degree of satisfaction. It is a maddening question, and much like the proverbial chicken and the egg, it isn't likely to be resolved.

People tell stories. People repeat stories. And as they repeat them, people modify stories, which sometimes results in the birth of new stories. There might have been some highly imaginative, creative people who invented stories at some point, but that sort of person has yet to be identified in the annals of folklore studies. Folklorists often asked renowned storytellers to tell a new story, to invent something that they had not heard. Without exception, these requests were refused by the storytellers who explained that while they repeated stories, they did not invent them. In general, it may be best to consider the possibility that the process of repetition and transmission is the source of much of the creativity that is evidenced in the international library of oral tradition.

One example may help shed light on the creative process: the Cornish droll tellers were known for their wild adaptation of the material they heard. Their counterparts in Ireland were the *seanchaithe*, professional storytellers who prided themselves in the faithful recitation of stories they had heard, as close to the original as possible. Perhaps in this, we can see the opportunity for new stories to be born, and indeed, Cornish oral tradition includes more than its fair share of distinct subtypes (i.e. variants) of legends and folktales, perhaps offering a hint as to how these things may come into existence.

And on whether there are real people or events behind legends, myths, and ancient gods:

When I see the posts like this asking about whether there were real people or events behind legends, myths, and/or the ancient gods, I respond with several observations. First, the idea that the gods and heroes of legend are based on real people had an early proponent in the Greek, late-fourth-century BCE writer, Euhemerus, giving his name to this approach to myth and legend: Euhemerism. Folklorists generally regard the idea that there was an actual basis for most oral tradition as barking up the wrong tree, because the original "real" event behind a story is usually elusive and searching for that core is a futile exercise. In addition, research into how stories began usually concludes that they emerge in a rather spontaneous way, typically without an actual incident to inspire them.

A few examples: the Classical Greek story of Perseus is an early manifestation of a widespread folktale, catalogued by the twentieth-century folklorists Antti Aarne and Stith Thompson as AT 300, "The Dragon Slayer." Was there a proto-Perseus who rescued a maiden from some sort of extraordinary threat or perhaps from some sort of human sacrifice? It is hard to answer that question, but it is not hard to imagine how far back in time that proto-incident would have had to occur: AT 300 is spread throughout Eurasia. It was collected from cultures that could have no conceivable literary connection with ancient Greece, and yet the shared assortment of motifs in the numerous variants clearly show some sort of genetic, that is, historically-connected relationship. Would we need, therefore, to go back thousands of years before the first recordation of the Perseus story to find this proto-Perseus? It is much easier to understand that the folktale simply diffused and that one of its manifestations was in ancient Greece.

Now, let's consider another example that has inspired a lot of spilled ink. A simple Google search for the "origins of King Arthur" provides more websites than one could easily read in a week. Was there a proto-Arthur? Perhaps. Maybe there were several. But what does that prove?

Every society has remarkable characters, and it may be a natural process for these sorts of individuals to attract all manner of traditional stories that have nothing to do with the original inspiration of the cycle of legends.

So, what do we have with Arthur? Was there a core source (or sources) for this legendary character? Let's concede for the sake of argument that the answer is yes. Now, did this individual have a great warrior at his side who became ensnared by the leader's wife in the fashion of Lancelot and Guinevere? That is more problematic since this type of story is also associated with Diarmuid and Grainne in the Irish court of King Finn and with the Cornish stories of Tristan and Isolde in the court of King Mark. One could even argue that it is the story behind Helen of Troy. In fact, it appears that this was a widespread type of story that became associated with various courts of historical legend. We cannot conclude that every great king had a queen who was attracted to one of his warriors and coerced him to take her away. This is simply a story that was attached to cycles involving great courts. In short, the further one goes back to find the "real Arthur," the less the candidate (or candidates) look like the King Arthur who has been beloved for centuries. The proto Arthurs are not really King Arthur. They may be seeds but they look nothing like the tree that would grow over the centuries. We do not hold an acorn and say "Ah, I have in my hand a mighty oak tree." It is not yet a tree. It is a seed. And the two look very different even if they are genetically linked.

One more example: there is a widespread legend told by countless families of the ghostly appearance of a loved one in anticipation of news that the individual died. This became a popular tradition in post-Famine Ireland because so many relatives lived in North America or elsewhere. But it is frequently told by all sorts of people internationally. So, we can ask, are there real-life, actual inspirations for this legend? That is, do the spirits of the dead actually come to visit loved ones? Well, how the hell should I know? To paraphrase a famous line from the television show "Star Trek," "Damn it Jim, I'm a folklorist, not a ghost hunter." And I have no intention of becoming a ghost hunter. It doesn't matter what is behind stories so much as it does that people tell these stories. I'm in it for that part of the game; I consider stories as they are told over time, to gain from that material some insight into the past, into culture, and into the human condition. I am a folklorist. And with that, my plate is full.

BIBLIOGRAPHY

Primary Sources

Note: Primary sources appear with a variety of translators, editors, and publishers. Serious researchers should secure complete, standard editions.

Afanas'ev, Aleksandr, translated by Norbert Guterman, *Russian Fairy Tales* (1945).

Arnason, Jón, *Icelandic Legends*, translated by George E. J. Powell and Eiríkur Magnússon (1864).

Ausabel, Nathan, *A Treasury of Jewish Folklore* (1948).

Bottrell, William, *Traditions of the Hearthside: Stories of West Cornwall: Series 1* (1870).
--------, *Traditions of the Hearthside: Stories of West Cornwall: Series 2* (1873).
--------, *Stories and Folklore of West Cornwall* (1880).

Bray, Anne Eliza, *A Peep at the Pixies, or Legends of the West* (1854).

Briggs, Katharine, *Folk Tales of Britain* (1971).

Brunvand, J. H., *Too Good to be True: The Colossal Book of Urban Legends* (1999; this compendium is excellent, but Brunvand has many other books dealing with urban legends).

Budge, E. A. Wallis, *The Book of the Dead* (1960).

Burton, Richard F., *The Arabian Nights* (1883).

Campbell, J. F., *Popular Tales of the West Highlands, I-IV* (2nd edition, 1890-1893).

Child, Francis James, *The English and Scottish Popular Ballads*, (1882 to 1898).

Christiansen, Reidar Th., *Folktales of Norway* (1964).

Coffin, Tristram P., and Hennig Cohen, editors, *Folklore in America* (1966).

Douglas, Ronald MacDonald, *Scottish Lore and Folklore* (1982).

Eberhard, Wolfram, ed., *Folktales of China* (1965).

Glassie, Henry, *Irish Folk History: Texts from the North* (1982).
--------, *Irish Folktales* (1985).

Graves, Robert, *The Greek Myths* (1955).

Grimm, Jacob and Wilhelm, *Kinder und Hausmärchen* (there are various editions and translations of Grimm's Fairytales, but the better sources have all 210 tales, number accordingly for research purposes).

Hollander, Lee M., translator, *The Poetic Edda* (1962).

Hoogasian-Villa, Susie, *One Hundred Armenian Tales and their Folkloristic Relevance* (1966).

Hunt, Robert, *Popular Romances of the West of England or the Drolls, Traditions, and Superstitions of Old Cornwall* (1903).

Institoris, Heinrich and Jacob Springer, *Malleus Maleficarum (The Witch Hammer)* (1487).

Johnson, Marjorie T., *Seeing Fairies: From the Lost Archives of the Fairy Investigation Society, Authentic Reports of Fairies in Modern Times* (2014).

Kirk, Robert, see Stewart, R. J.

Kvideland, Reimund and Henning K. Sehmsdorf, editors, *Scandinavian Folk Belief and Legend* (Minneapolis, Minnesota, 1988).

Lindow, John, *Swedish Legends and Folktales* (1978).

O'Sullivan, Sean, *Folktales of Ireland* (1966).

Parry-Jones, D., *Welsh Legends and Fairy Lore* (1992).

Perrault, Charles, *Histoires ou Contes du temps passé* (1697, Histories, or Tales of Past Times, numerous translations).

Ross, Anne, *The Folklore of the Scottish Highlands* (1976).

Sayers, Peig, *Peig: The Autobiography of Peig Sayers of the Great Blasket Island*, translated by Bryan MacMahon (1974).
--------, *An Old Woman's Reflections: The Life of a Blasket Island Storyteller* (1962).

Simpson, Jacqueline, translator and editor, *Icelandic Folktales and Legends* (1972).
--------, *The Penguin Book of Scandinavian Folktales* (1994).

Snorri Sturluson, *The Prose Edda: Tales from Norse Mythology*, translated by Jean I. Young (1954).

Stewart, R. J., *Robert Kirk: Walker between Worlds*, a new edition of *The Secret Commonwealth of Elves, Fauns and Fairies* (1990).

Swire, Otta F., *The Outer Hebrides and their Legends* (1966).

Tregarthen, Enys, *North Cornwall Fairies and Legends* (1906).

Secondary Sources

(Many of the following include a great deal of primary source material.)

Aarne, Antti and Stith Thompson, *The Types of the Folktale: A Classification and Bibliography* (second revision, 1987); revised: Hans-Jörg Uther, *The Types of International Folktales: A Classification and Bibliography, Based on the System of Antti Aarne and Stith Thompson* (2004).

Adorno, Theodor W., *In Search of Wagner* (1984).

Almqvist, Bo, edited by Éilís Ní Dhuibhne and Séamas Ó Catháin, *Viking Ale: Studies on Folklore Contacts between the Northern and the Western Worlds* (1991).

Axelrod, Alan, and Harry Oster, *The Penguin Dictionary of American Folklore* (2000).

Bächman, Louise and Åke Hultkrantz, *Studies in Lapp Shamanism* (1978).

Baughman, Ernest W., *A Type and Motif Index of the Folktales of England and North America* (1966).

Bettelheim, Bruno, *The Uses of Enchantment: The Meaning and Importance of Fairy Tales* (1975).

Bourke, Angela, *The Burning of Bridget Cleary: A True Story* (1999).

Briggs, Katharine, *The Anatomy of Puck* (1959).
--------, *An Encyclopedia of Fairies, Hobgoblins, Brownies, Bogies, and Other Supernatural Creatures* (1976).
--------, *The Fairies in Tradition and Literature* (1967).

Bronner, Simon J., "Practice Theory in Folklore and Folklife Studies," *Folklore*, 123:1:23-47 (2012).

Brungéus, Nils-Arvid, *Carl Wilhelm von Sydow: A Swedish Pioneer in Folklore* (2009).

Brunvand, J. H., *A Study and Research Guide* (1976).
--------, *The Study of American Folklore* (1968).

Christiansen, Reidar Th., *European Folklore in American* (1962).
--------, *The Migratory Legends: A Proposed List of Types with a Systematic Catalogue of the Norwegian Variants* (1958).

Cocchiara, Giuseppe, 1981, *The History of Folklore in Europe*, Institute for the Study of Human Issues; English translation by John N. McDaniel, *Storia del folklore in Europa* (1971).

Cochrane, Timothy, "The Concept of Ecotypes in American Folklore," *Journal of Folklore Research*, 24:1 (Jan-Apr 1987).

Darnton, Robert, *The Great Cat Massacre and Other Episodes in French Cultural*

History (1985).

D'Azevedo, Warren L., volume editor, *Handbook of North American Indians: Volume 11* (1986).

Delargy, Seamus (J. H. Delargy), "The Gaelic Story-Teller with some notes on Gaelic Folk-Tales" (1946, reprinted in Dundes, 1999).

Demos, John Putnam, *Entertaining Satan: Witchcraft and the Culture of Early New England* (1982).

Dorson, R. M., *History of British Folklore, Volume I: The British Folklorists* (1968).
--------, "The Question of Folklore in a New Nation," *Journal of the Folklore Institute* 3:3 (December 1966).

Dundes, Alan, *International Folkloristics: Classic Contributions by the Founders of Folklore* (1999).
--------, *The Morphology of the North American Indian Folktales* (1964).
--------, *The Study of Folklore* (1965).

Ellis Davidson, H. R., *Gods and Myths of Northern Europe* (1964).

Evans, E. Estyn, *Irish Folkways* (1957).

Evans-Wentz, Walter Yeeling, *The Fairy Faith in Celtic Countries* (1911).

Fish, Lydia, "The European background of American miners' beliefs," in *Folklore Studies in Honour of Herbert Halpert*, ed. Kenneth S. Goldstein and Neil V. Rosenberg (1980).

Frazer, J. G., *The Golden Bough* (1913).

Glassie, Henry, *Passing the Time in Ballymenone* (1982).

Green, Miranda, *Dictionary of Celtic Myth and Legend* (1992).

Greenway, John, ed., *Folklore of the Great West* (1969).

Grimm, Jacob, *Deutsche Mythologie (Teutonic Mythology*, 1835, numerous translations).
--------, *Deutsche Sagen (Teutonic Legends*, 1816-1818, numerous translations).

Hale, Amy and Philip Payton, editors, *New Directions in Celtic Studies* (2000).

Hamerow, Theodore S. *The Social Foundations of German Unification, 1858-1871* (1969)

Hand, Wayland, "California Miner's Folklore: Above Ground" and "California Miner's Folklore: Below Ground," *California Folklore Quarterly* 1 (1942) 24-46 and 127-153.

Hartmann, Elisabeth, *Die Trollvorstellungen in den Sagen und Märchen der Skandinavischen Völker* (1936).

Henderson, Lizanne and Edward J. Cowan, *Scottish Fairy Belief* (2001).

Hobsbawm, Eric and Terence Ranger, eds., *The Invention of Tradition* (1983).

Hoffman-Krayer, E., and Hanns Büchtold-Stäubli, *Handwörterbuch des deutschen Aberglaudens* (1927-1941).

Hopkin, David, "The Ecotype, Or a Modest Proposal to Reconnect Cultural and Social History," from Melissa Calaresu, Filippo de Vivo, and Joan-Pau Rubiés, editors, *Exploring Cultural History: Essays in Honour of Peter Burke* (2012) 31-54.

Hultkrantz, Åke, *The Supernatural Owners of Nature* (1961).

Ikeda, Hiroko, *A Type and Motif Index of Japanese Folk-Literature* (1971).

Jackson, Kenneth Hurlstone, *The Oldest Irish Tradition: A Window on the Iron Age* (1984).

James, Ronald M., "Cornish Folklore: Context and Opportunity," *Cornish Studies 18*, ed. by Philip Payton (2011).
--------, "Knockers, Knackers, and Ghosts: Immigrant Folklore in the Western Mines," *Western Folklore Quarterly* 51:2 (April 1992).
--------, "'The Spectral Bridegroom': A Study in Cornish Folklore," *Cornish Studies 20*, ed. by Philip Payton (2013).
--------, *Trolls: From Scandinavia to Dam Dolls, Tolkien, and Harry Potter* (2014).

Karlson, Carol F., *The Devil in the Shape of a Woman: Witchcraft in Colonial New England* (1987).

Kiefer, Emma Emily, *Albert Wesselski and Recent Folktale Theories* (1973).

Kittredge, George Lyman, *Witchcraft in Old and New England* (1928).

Koch, John T., *Celtic Culture: A Historical Encyclopedia* (2005).

Kohn, Hans, *The Idea of Nationalism: A Study in Its Origins and Background* (1944).

Kramer, Samuel Noah, *Mythologies of the Ancient World* (1961).

Krohn, Kaarle, translated by Roger L. Welsch, *Folklore Methodology: Formulated by Julius Krohn and expanded by Nordic Researchers* (1971).

Kvideland, Reimund and Henning K. Sehmsdorf, editors, *Nordic Folklore: Recent Studies* (1989).

Luomala, Katharine, *The Menehune of Polynesia and other Mythical Little People of Oceania* (1951).

Leach, Maria, *Dictionary of Folklore, Mythology and Legend* (1949).

Levi-Strauss, Claude, *The Savage Mind* (1966).
--------, *Structural Anthropology* (1963).

Liljeblad, Sven S., *Introduction to Folklore: Elementary Forms of Popular Tradition* (1966).
--------, "Oral Tradition: Content and Style of Verbal Arts," in D'Azevedo
--------, *Die Tobiageschichte und andere Märchen mit Toten Helfern* (1927).

Lüthi, Max, *The European Folktale: Form and Nature* (1986).

Lysaght, Patricia, *The Banshee: The Irish Death Messenger* (1986).

Manning, Paul, "The Pixies' Progress: How the Pixy became part of the 19th Century Fairy Mythology," in Michael Dylan Foster and Jeffrey Tolbert, eds. *The Folkloresque: Reframing Folklore in a Popular Culture World* (anticipated 2015).

McGlathery, James M., ed., *The Brothers Grimm and Folktale* (1988).

MacKillop, James, *A Dictionary of Celtic Mythology* (1998).

Narváez, Peter, ed., *The Good People: New Fairylore Essays* (1997).

Odstedt, Ella, *Varulven i svensk folktradition* (1943).

Ó hÓgáin, Dáithí, *The Lore of Ireland: An Encyclopedia of Myth, Legend and Romance* (2006).
--------, "Migratory Legends in Medieval Irish Literature, *Béaloideas* 60/61 (1992/1993) 57-74.

Orenstein, Catherine, *Little Red Riding Hood Uncloaked: Sex, Morality, and the Evolution of a Fairy Tale* (2008).

Ó Súilleabháin, Seán, *Handbook of Irish Folklore* (1966).
--------, and Reidar Th. Christiansen, *The Types of the Irish Folktale* (1967).

Pentijäinen, Juha, "The Dead without Status," from Reimund Kvideland and Henning K. Sehmsdorf, editors, *Nordic Folklore: Recent Studies* (1989).

Propp, Vladímir, *Morphology of the Folktale*, translated by Laurence Scott and revised and edited by Louis A. Wagner (1968, originally 1928).

Rank, Otto, *The Myth of the Birth of the Hero and Other Writings* (1932).

Simpson, Jacqueline, "Repentant Soul or Walking Corpse? Debatable Apparitions in Medieval England," *Folklore*, 114:3 (December 2003) 389-402.
--------, and Steve Roud, *A Dictionary of English Folklore* (2000).

Strömbäck, Dag, *Folklore och filologi* (1970).

Swahn, Jan-Öjvind, *The Tale of Cupid and Psyche* (1955).

Taylor, Archer, *English Riddles from Oral Traditions* (1951).
--------, *The Proverb, and an Index to the Proverb* (1962).

Tehrani, Jamshid J., "The Phylogeny of Little Red Riding Hood," PLOS/ONE, November 13, 2013 (online journal accessed November 15, 2013: http://www.plosone.org/article/info%3Adoi%2F10.1371%2Fjournal.pone.0078871).

Thomas, Keith, *Religion and the Decline of Magic* (London: Folio Society, 2012, originally published in 1971; second edition in 1991, minor changes in the 2012 edition).

Thompson, Stith, *The Folktale* (1977).
--------, *Motif-Index of Folk-Literature: Revised and Enlarged Edition* (1955).

Uí Ógaín, Ríonach and Anne O'Connor, "'Spor ar An gCois Is gan An Chos Ann': A Study of 'The Dead Lover's Return' in Irish Tradition" *Béaloideas*, volume 51 (1983) 126-144.

Uther, Hans-Jörg, see Aarne, Antti.

Von Sydow, Carl Wilhelm, *Selected Papers on Folklore* edited by Laurits Bødker (1948).

Warner, Marina, *From the Beast to the Blonde: Fairy Tales and Their Tellers* (London, 1994).

Wilson, William A., "Herder, Folklore and Romantic Nationalism," *Journal of Popular Culture* 6:4 (1973) 819-835.

Zimmermann, George Denis, *The Irish Storyteller* (2001).

Zipes, Jack, *Breaking the Magic Spell: Radical Theories of Folk and Fairy Tales* (1979).
--------, *The Brothers Grimm: From Enchanted Forests to the Modern World* (2002).
--------, *Fairy Tale as Myth: Myth as Fairy Tale* (1994).
--------, *The Irresistible Fairy Tale: The Cultural and Social History of a Genre* (2012).
--------, *Spells of Enchantment: The Wondrous Fairy Tales of Western Cultures* (1991).
--------, *Victorian Fairy Tales: The Revolt of the Fairies and Elves* (1987).

INDEX

Aarne, Antti, 13, 60-61, 68, 70, 74, 124
Abduction, supernatural; see Changelings
African American folklore, 41-42
Agriculture, 20
Aladdin's lamp, 89
All Saint's Day, 33-34
All Soul's Day, 33-34
Allingham, William, 102
Alphabet, 21-22
American Indians, ix, 11, 13-14, 21, 27, 47, 63, 65
Aphrodite, 54, 55, 57
Aquae Sulis, 85-87, *86*
Arabic folklore, 26, 29, 120
Ares, 54, 55
Arnason, Jón, 119
Arthur, King, 19, 49, 89, 124-5
Astrology, 27, 28
Athena, 54, 55, 57
Autumn, see Seasons
Babylonia, see Mesopotamia
Balkans, 53
Ballads, 5, 6-7, 69-70
Bears in folklore, 24, 75
Beltane, 32
Beowulf, 97
Berserkers, 83-84, *84*
Bettelheim, Bruno, 15-16
Bible, 56, 88, 95, 96, 121
Birds, 6, 43, 46, 49, 63

Bjarki, Bothvar, 75
Black Death, 81-82
Blind motif, 88
Boaz, Franz, viii, 11
Boogey man, 6
Brentano, Clemens, 114, 115-7, 120, 121-2
Brigantia (Celtic goddess), *30*
Brigit, Saint, 29-31, *30*, *31*
Britain, 33-34, 49, 50, *54*, 77, 80, 89, 101, 115
Brunvand, Jan Harold, 106-7, 123
Bull of heaven, 21-22
Bürger, Gottfried August, 74
Calendar, folklore related to the, 26-40
Campbell, Joseph, 14-15
Cattle, 17, 32, 49-50
Celtic folklore, *8*, 19, 29-32, 34, 39, *86*
Changelings, 44, 68-69, 80-81
Child, F. J., 70
Childbirth, 42-44
Christianity, 27-28, 32-33, 35, 44, 49-51, 73, 89, 92-104
Christiansen, Reidar Th., 69, 77, 83, 94, 96, 98, 99
Christmas, 20, 27, 34, 35-36, 37, 39-40, 46, 48
Churches, 19, 30, 42, 44, *54*, 68, 97, 99
Churching, 44
Cill Dara, 30
Cities underground/underwater, 89
Clockwise, 18-19, 24
Colors, 20-21, 44
Conspiracy Theories, 107-8
Cornish folklore, 13, 49, 73, 87, 100-1, 124, 125
Counterclockwise, see Clockwise
Crossroads, 36, 41-42, 47
Daedalus, 59
Dame World, 94-95, 99-100
Day of the Dead, 34
Death, 19, 21, 22, 29, 33-34, 35, 37, 38-39, 42, 44-46, 55, 68, 72, 73-76, 77-78, 81-82, 88
Delargy, James, 66
Denmark, 79, 119-20
Devil, 19, 22, 34, 40, 41-42, 50, 76, 85, 89, 92, 96, 97
Diana (goddess), 55, 76
Diarmuid and Grainne, 125
Directions, 19
Disney films, 68, 78
Dite, 67-68
Divination, 47-51, *48*
Dragons, 63, 89-90, 124

Dreams, 14, 29, 47-48, 75, 82-83, 98, 102
Droll tellers, see storytellers
Dundes, Alan, 13-14, 15, 65, 108-9, 125
East, see Directions
Easter, 20, 32
Ecotype Method, viii, 11-12, 67, 101
Edda, Poetic, 74
Edda, Prose, 118
Egyptians, 21, 27, 28, 75, 108
Elements, the four, 20
Elves, see Fairies and elves, and related supernatural beings
Epic Laws of Folk Narrative, 62-65
Etiological legends, 5, 68, 87, 121
Euhemerus, 124
Eyrbyggja Saga, 99
Fairies, elves, and related supernatural beings, 19, 24, 39-40, 57-59, 68-69, 80-81, 90, 96-97, 102-4, *103*
Fairytale, definition, 4-5; see also Folktale
Familiars, 85, 87
Fates/Fortuna, 55, 88
Fatima, 54-55
Feigr, 45
Feilberg, Henning Frederik, 67
Fichte, Johann Gottlieb, 114
Fict, 6, 40, 43
Finland, 17
Finnish Historic Geographic method, viii, 10-13, 65, 66, 67
First and last, 23
Fisher, Walter, 112
Flood, the Great, *58*, 68, 121
Flying Dutchman, 89
Folk ballad, 5
Folklore, and belief, 17-25; definition, 1-3
Folktale, definition, 4; methodology, 10-16; genre, 60-66
Foo-fighters, 105
Fortunetelling, 43
Foundation sacrifice, 41
Freud, Sigmund, 14-15
Freya, 28, 57
Futhark, 22
Geasa, 23
Gender, 42, 66, 70-71
Germanic folklore, 22, 26-28, 37-39, 44, 56
Germany, 17, 24, 50, 92-95, 114-7
Ghosts, souls, and the walking dead, 29, 45-46, 72, 73-75, 88, 90, 99, 101, 107, 125
Giants, 56, 73, 86-88, 89-90
Gilgamesh, 85-87, 121

Gnomes, 39, 104
Gnomes (book), 104
Grateful Dead, viii, 7, 67
Greeks, 21-22, 26, 27, 41, 53, 56, 85, 125
Gremlins, 73, 106-7
Grimm, Jacob, 2, 61, 115-20, 121
Grimm's Fairytales (various titles), 2, 68, 117, 120
Guntram legend, 97-98
Guy Fawkes Day, 34
Hadrian's Wall, *8*
Halloween, 27, 33-34
Hamerow, Theodore S., 117
Harry Potter, 80
Hartmann (Hofelich-Hartmann), Elisabeth, viii, 1, 67
Hawaii, 23
Hearth, the, 40, 41, 55
Helen of Troy, 125
Hephaestus, 59
Hera, 54, 55, 57
Herder, Johann Gottfried, 114-5, 117-19, 121
Historic Geographic method, see Finnish Historic Geographic method
Historical legends, 69
Hitler, Adolph, 7, 12, 22, 65
Homo Narrans, 112
Horses in folklore, 35, 36, 40, 41, 42, 56-57, 69, 74, 76-77, 90
Hulderfolk and related Scandinavian entities, 24, 80, 91; see also Trolls and *Rå*
Iceland, 36, 39, 45, 47, 58, 80, 83, 88, 99, 118-9
Immigration, 92-104
Indo-European languages and folk belief, 7-9, 12, 22, 42, 53, 56, 62, 65, 67
Industrialization, 10, 26-27, 92-104
Innocent VIII, Pope, 50
Internet lore, see Web lore
Irish folklore, 6, 9, 13, 19, 23, 24, 29-31, 33-34, 36, *38*, *48*, 49, 50, *54*, 61, 66, 78, 80, 87, 101, 102, 106, 120, 124, 125
Iron and the supernatural, 41, 43
Isis (goddess), 54
Jack-'o-Lantern, 33-34
Jackson, President Andrew, 68
Japanese folklore, 61, 99
Jesus, 35-36, *58*, 88-89
Jewish folk culture, 27, 98
John, Saint, see Midsummer's Day
Johnson, Robert, 42
Jokes as folklore, 61, 70-71, 111
Jung, Carl Gustav, 14-15
Jupiter (Roman god), 28, 55, 56
Kirk, Robert, 102

Knockers, 73, 100-1
Kohn, Hans, 115
Kramer, Heinrich, 50
Krampus, 35
Ladurie, Emmanuel LeRoy, 97-98
Lancelot and Guinevere, 125
Land dead versus sea dead legend, 98-99
Left and right, 18-19
Legend, definition, 3-4, 5; genre, 61-62, 67-69, 94-101
Lemmings, 68
Lenore Legend, 74, 92, 100
Letters, see Alphabet
Liljeblad Sven S., vii-ix, 18, 27, 47, 67, 72
MacPherson, James, 116-7
Magic, 17-25, 28-29, 32, 33, 36, 41, 42, 43, 44, 46, 49-51, 52, 53, 56, 61, 75, 82-85, 103
Magpies, 49
Malinowski, Bronislaw, 11
Malleus Maleficarum, 50
Märchen, see Folktales
Marie de France, 84-85
Marriage, 17, 24, 42, 44, 68
Mars (Roman god), 28, 55
Martin, Saint, 34-35
Martin Luther, 81
Mary, the Virgin, 20, 54-55, *58*
May Day, 32
Maypole, 32
Medieval folklore, 5, 6, 19-21, 23, 27, 29, 31, 35, 45-46, 49-50, 54-55, 69, 74, 85-87, 88-100, 118-9
Medusa, 64, 85-87, *86*
Memorates, 68, 107
Mercury (Roman god), 28
Mermaids, 77-78, *77*, 90
Mesopotamia, 2, 27, 28-29, 85-87
Mexican folklore, 34
Michael, Saint, 32-33
"A Midsummer Night's Dream," 102
Midsummer's Day, 32
Midwife and the Fairies, legend, 81
Migratory legends, see Testimonial legends; and see Christiansen, Reidar Th.
Mithraism, 28, 35, 37
Modernization, 10
Montaillou: The Promised Land of Error, see Ladurie, Emmanuel LeRoy
Moon, 20, 27, 28
Morgan le Fey, 49
Mother goddess, 53-55, 57

Motif, definition, 6
Mythology, definition, 5-6; ancient and medieval, 52-59
Nationalism, 114-20
Native Americans; see American Indian
Navaho, 21
New Grange, *38*
New Year's Eve, 27, 36-37, 39, 77
Nicholas, Saint, 35
Niccor, 40, 42
Nightmare, 82-83
Nisse, 39-40, 79-80
Noa, 23, 81
North, see Directions
Northern Paiutes, ix, 87
Norway, 60, 67, 68, 80, 118-20
Nosferatu, 45
Numbers, 21
Odin, 22, 28, 42, 56, 63
Odstedt, Ella, 83
Oicotype method, see Ecotype method
Olrik, Axel, 62-65, 67, 70
One-Strophic Folk Lyric, 70
Opposites, 23, 25
Orenstein, Catherine, 66
Owners of nature, supernatural, 72-73
Paiutes; see Northern Paiutes
Pan, 55, 85, 87
Paúngaa'a, see Water baby
Pentagram, 22
Perrault, Charles, 120
Perseus, 64, 85, 86, 124
Peter, Saint, 34
Pictish stones, 78, *79*
Pied Piper of Hamlin, 40
Planets, 28
Polyphemus legend, 76, 94
Poppy or the Adventures of a Fairy, *103*
Poseidon, 42, 54, 55, 56
Positivism, 11
Pregnancy, 42-44
Propp, Vladímir, 12-14, 65-66
Psychology and folklore, 14-16
Puck, 87, 102
Pythagoreans, 21
Rå, 76, 92-93
Rabbits in folklore, 43, 85
Reddit.com, ix, 123

Riddles, *58*, 70
Right and left, see Left and right
Romans, 22, 27, 29, 33, 35, 37, 48, 56, 82
Rowse, A. L., 49
Russia, 24, 27, 35, 60, 67, 72, 79, 80, 120
Sacrifices, 34, 40, 41-42, 53, 56, 86, 96, 124
Sagen, see Legends
Samhain, 33
Santa Claus, 6, 37, 39-40
Satan, see Devil
Saturn (Roman god), 28, 55, 56
Saturnalia, 35, 37
Satyricon, 81, 83
Sayers, Peig, 66
Scandinavia, 19, 24, 39-40, 42, 50, 94-95; see also Denmark; Finland; Norway; and Sweden
Seanchaithe, see Storytellers
Seasons, 27-28, 29-40
Semitic alphabet and folklore, 21, 56, 60, 62, see also Jewish folk culture
Shamanism, 23, 24, 47, 52, 87
Sidhe, see Fairies and elves
Siegfried, 63
Sigurdsson, Jón, 119
Síleagh-na-gig, 54
Sleeping army, 88
Sleipnir, 42, 56
Snorri Sturluson, 118-9
South, see Directions
Sprenger, Jacob, 50
Spring, see Seasons
Stations of the Cross, 19
Stonehenge, 37-38
Stork, the, 6, 43
Storytellers, 13-14, 123-4
Sumerian culture, see Mesopotamia
Summer, see Seasons
Sun, 18, 19, 22, 27, 28, 29, 37, 38
Swastika, 22
Swedish folklore, 76, 79, 80, 87, 120
Swedish School, see Ecotype method
Sydow, Carl Wilhelm von, see Von Sydow, Carl Wilhelm
Tabu/taboos, 23-24, 29, 40, 43, 81
Taurus, see Bull of heaven
Thompson, Stith, 13, 60, 68, 124
Thoms, William, 1
Thor, 28, 56, 64
Testimonial legends, 68-69

Tir na nOg, 19
Tiw/Týr, 28, 56
Tolkien, 121-2; ring, 89
Tommyknockers, see Knockers
Tomte, see *Nisse*
Tooth fairy, 6
Trick-or-treat, 34
Trickster, 39, 40, 87, 97
Trinities among deities, *8*, 54, 57
Tristan and Isolde, 125
Trolls, 4, 67, 68, 80, 90
Twelve Days of Christmas, 35-36; see also Christmas
Twiddling thumbs, 18
Type, 13, definition, 6, 60-61
UFOs, 89, 105-6
Unicorns, 91
Urban folklore, 105-113, 123
Uther, Hans-Jörg, 60
Valentine, Saint, 31
Vampires, 45
Vanishing Hitchhiker, 107
Variant, definition, 7
Venus (Roman god), 28
Virginity, 44
von Arnim, Achim, 114, 115-7, 120, 121-2
von Savigny, Friedrich, Karl, 115, 116
von Sydow, Carl Wilhelm, viii, 6, 11-12, 67-69, 101, 107
Vulcan, 59
Wagner, Richard, 117
Walking dead; see Ghosts and the walking dead
Walpurgis, Saint, see May Day
Wandering Jew, 89
Water baby, 87
Water sprites, 72; see also mermaids
Wayland the Smith, 57-59, *58*
Web Lore, 60, 106-7, 108-11, *109*, *110*, *112*
Weekdays, 28-29
Wells in folklore, 42
Werewolf, 82-85
West, see Directions
Wild Hunt, 89
Wild man, 85-87
Will-'o-the-Wisp, 33-34, 89
Winter, see Seasons
Witch bottle, 51
Witchcraft, 42, 47-51, 82, 84
Woden, see Odin

Xerox lore, 60, 108-10, *109*, *110*
Yule, see Christmas
Zeus, 54, 55, 56
Zipes, Jack, 116-7
Zodiac, 27, 29
Zombies; see Ghosts and the walking dead
Zwarte Piet, 35

Made in the USA
Middletown, DE
18 July 2017